MADE

HOLY

John Griswold, series editor

Made Holy

ESSAYS

Emily Arnason Casey

*The University of
Georgia Press*
ATHENS

Published by the University of Georgia Press
Athens, Georgia 30602
www.ugapress.org
© 2019 by Emily Arnason Casey
All rights reserved
Designed by Kaelin Chappell Broaddus
Set in 11.6/14 Fournier MT Std by Kaelin Chappell Broaddus
Printed and bound by Sheridan Books, Inc.
The paper in this book meets the guidelines for permanence
and durability of the Committee on Production Guidelines
for Book Longevity of the Council on Library Resources.

Most University of Georgia Press titles are
available from popular e-book vendors.

Printed in the United States of America

19 20 21 22 23 P 5 4 3 2 1

Library of Congress Cataloging-in-Publication Data

Names: Casey, Emily Arnason, 1979– author.
Title: Made holy : essays / by Emily Arnason Casey.
Description: Athens : The University of Georgia Press, [2019] |
Includes bibliographical references.
Identifiers: LCCN 2019008101| ISBN 9780820355993 (paperback : alk. paper) |
ISBN 9780820355986 (e-book)
Subjects: LCSH: Casey, Emily Arnason, 1979– | Casey, Emily Arnason, 1979––Family.
Classification: LCC CT275.C3427 A3 2019 | DDC 808.84—dc23
LC record available at https://lccn.loc.gov/2019008101

For My Family

What we believe is the inner voice
that proves to us that we exist.

—JUDITH KITCHEN

Contents

The Cabin

Before my parents sold the Burnt Shanty Lake cabin the year I turned thirty, I sometimes went there alone. It was down the road a mile or so from my grandparents' cabin, where my mother had spent her childhood summers and my aunt, uncle, and cousins stayed during the summer. One afternoon, my first summer home from college, I made the forty-minute drive from my parents' house to visit it. I parked the car at the top of the steep and winding driveway. The grass between the tire ruts grew to my knees. Birch and poplar trees stood tall. The quiet, cut only by the choir of birds, eased me. I carried a notebook and pen, and though I daydreamed about spending a month there with just a typewriter and a stack of books, I never stayed long. After a day spent immersed in solitude, as night hinted at the sky, I'd long for the noise of my large family, the traffic of daily life.

In the cabin, the window slid open. I found a rag and wiped the table. Cans of beans and jars of peanut butter were stacked beside bottles of bug spray and shampoo in a wooden cupboard my father had made. I left my notebook on the table and walked down to the dock; it groaned and swayed as I made my way to the end. I sat and looked down into the water. Both sides were weedy now, though the lily pads had not yet made their way to the swimming side of the dock. The island seemed so close, as though I might dive off the end of the dock and surface at its shore. My sisters and I had spent hours swimming back and forth to the island as girls, careful to never let our toes stray too deep and graze the weeds that lay at the bottom of the shallow parts of the lake.

From the dock, the cabin looked rundown: the red paint had faded and moss grew in places on the roof. Long, wispy grass bowed in the breeze. The front of the cabin stood on cinder blocks, which left a large crawl space. Lumber and lawn chairs and old toys collected there, along with perhaps a beat-up lawnmower. As soon as we arrived at the cabin for a stay, my father liked to cut the grass. The job of collecting the sticks in the yard so he could mow was preferred to sweeping and mopping the cabin floors or making beds and unpacking groceries. Other than a few pines my father had planted, the yard was filled with birch that grew tall into the sky. As a younger man, my father pole-climbed them to hang swings or once an enormous Styrofoam bear as a joke.

In ten years, my parents would sell the cabin they had bought the year after I, their first child, was born. And though we had only lived there during the summers, it was our first permanent home. The new owners would tear it down and rebuild. Perhaps they paved the impossible driveway that we had avoided navigating for fear of losing a muffler on one of our used cars, parking instead at the top of the hill and hiking in our stuff: coolers, blankets, bedding, paper bags of groceries, extra fuel for the lanterns, chubby paperbacks, and playing cards. By the time they sold the cabin we hadn't spent a significant amount of time there for at least fifteen years, and more recently, we had barely made a single summer visit. But it remained a nest of memory for me. My childhood tethered to its homey comforts.

᷒᷒᷒᷒

The sunlight caught in the tall grass as I ran down the hill from the cabin to the lake. Ten years old, I chose my steps carefully in order to avoid hurting my feet on rough patches of grass or sharp sticks. I always ran the hill. Walking felt entirely a waste of time. The lake reflected sky and stood still in the morning light. An occasional breeze washed off its surface with a quiver. I stood alone beside the water waiting for someone to join me before slipping

from the dock into the lake. Morning smelled and sounded different than any other part of the day: the angle of the sun and the
chorus of birds, the soft comfort of a well-rested body, new with
morning and youth, vibrant and eager, made it the best part of the
day. All that long summer of my tenth year, the water of the lake
offered relief from the heat and pleasure. I made an offering of my
body, diving in, swimming long, floating on my back, watching
the white, sun-crested clouds drift above. While on the hill, the
cabin stood like a secret guardian of my inner world.

The cabin's red outer walls and big front windows faced the
lake. From the beach, I looked up at the windows. I could see my
mom in the loft standing over her bed, smoothing out the covers.
My feet in the sand felt cool, and the smell of the hot sun baking
the grass lingered in the breeze, creating that particular smell of
summer at the cabin. I walked to the end of the wooden dock and
peered down into water, tinted a sage green. Around the swimming side of the dock the bottom of the lake was sandy, but the
other side was thick with weeds, its surface covered in slick green
lily pads. I stood alone looking into the murky waters of the lake
and then out across the water to the tiny island. Further, to the
opposite shores with their tiny cabins, miniature speedboats, or
smoke coiling from the chimneys of saunas in the evening.

I looked back at the cabin where my father was opening the sliding window he'd salvaged from his grandma's house. Diamond-
shaped cut glass fashioned a mosaic belt across the top of the window; it slid back and forth on metal tracks. Contrasted with the
sparseness of the rest of the cabin—its uninsulated walls and rus-
tic furniture Dad scavenged from the open-pit dump nearby—it
seemed a treasure.

"Dad!" I yelled, "Dad, are you coming?"

He looked through the window. "Go ahead, just stay close to
the dock," he called back.

My feet curled around the rough wooden edge of the dock. I
bent my knees, then launched myself out over the water. My hands
in prayer above my head cut the water upon entry. Underwater, I

kicked once, twice, and then surfaced too far beyond the dock. But
no one was looking at me through the cabin windows, so I ducked
down and swam out further, the water growing cooler with depth.
On the floor of the lake, green weeds undulated over hidden trea-
sures: lost toys, sunglasses, Mom's empty bottles of LaCroix min-
eral water tipped and blown in by the wind. I swam along the surface, careful never to let my foot kick deep enough to touch the
bed of mossy weeds.

With no one watching, I floated on my back staring up at the sky
imagining I was someone else. I liked to pretend to be the character from whatever book I was reading, to dream these other worlds
pressed into my own. I got out, spread my towel over the dock, and
lay down to warm myself in the sun. My sister Hannah appeared,
interrupting my game of make believe. "Can I share your towel,
Em?" she asked.

I looked up at her, feigning distress, "Where's yours?"

She shrugged. Without waiting for my response, she sat down
at the end of the dock, away from my towel.

"Wanna come swimming with me, Em?"

"I just went swimming," I said and rolled over onto my side
to look at her. She was chubbier than me and cuter. Her hair was
blond and curly, and she wore a blue swimsuit with a white ruffle.
During the years before she entered school and received speech
therapy, I acted as her translator. Frequent ear infections had pro-
duced a slight speech impediment in her. Hannah would start to
speak with confidence and then noticing the confusion in someone's face, her voice would trail off. I explained.

But she was eight now and her speech had improved.

"You go. Dad said we could go in if we stayed by the dock."

"No, I just wait for Mom," she said and turned away from me.

We would be close our entire lives, not because we spoke daily
to each other (though sometimes we did), shared intimacies,
and lived in the same town, but from a sisterly need: a desire to
cleave—both to cling and to cut away from each other. She was
my first sister, my first love and envy.

We returned every year to the cabin on Burnt Shanty Lake and spent the summer. Though we moved often then (my father going to school in North Dakota, then taking a job in West Virginia), the cabin remained our constant summer home, a place to retreat from the world. It was a world apart, without a phone, a television, or even electricity and running water. The cabin shaped our closeness as a family; we built up our tolerance of each other all summer in such tight quarters. But at age ten, in the crowd of my family—I was the oldest of five girls, and my brother would be born in three years—I began to long for singular selfhood. My mother's pregnancies with my fourth sister and later my brother felt insulting to me as a child, not the welcome surprise my parents might have hoped for. I knew better than to reveal this, however. As the oldest child, I had an acute awareness of my parents' emotions and a sense of responsibility for them. Once I had lightheartedly insulted my mother's wedding dress while looking at photos of her wedding; I found the visible pain it caused my mother unbearable. "That really hurt my feelings," she later told me. Perhaps because it was one of the first times I felt I had betrayed her or because I didn't really mean what I had said, but was trying on a snobby persona as children do, I carried the shame of my error for years. I had let her down. She rarely let me see that part of her. But how effective the truth is to a child. How confusing to try and translate the secret shame of grown-ups.

≈≈≈≈

I stood on the side of the steep hill looking down at the lily pad swamp. I held the coarse rope of the saucer swing that dangled from the upper reaches of a leaning birch. Swinging drew calluses along my upper palm. At night in bed, falling asleep, I liked to run my fingers over them. A small knot in the rope, two feet above the seat, provided a place to grip. I wrapped my legs around the seat, leaned into the hill, grabbed the knot, and sat down. Airborne over the lily pad swamp, I held my breath until the swing reached its full outward suspension and turned back toward land. The more I swung, and it became a compulsion for a day or two at a time, the more daring I became. I let my head hang back so that my shoulder-length hair fell loose or I'd straighten my arms and lean back, point one leg in the direction of the sky. Below, frogs hopped from the warm mud of shore onto the lily pads. Water lilies bloomed like white teacups. I was a fearless trapeze artist swinging over a lake of snakes in a sparkling costume of red and blue sequins or Anne of Green Gables giving Gilbert the cold shoulder, running home to help Matthew. I was Cassie Logan, defiant and proud as she faced injustice.

One day in the middle of July that summer, Dad walked up and down the hill for hours pushing a wheelbarrow filled with sand from the sandpit at the top of the driveway. He dumped the sand along the shore of the lake. It was only a quarter mile, but the hill was steep. His brown hair was streaked with blond and wet with sweat, his body muscled and tan. He wore old running shoes with holes in the toe and loose laces. Every time he came by I'd shout, "Come swing, Dad!" And he'd say, "In a little bit," and tromp back up the hill determined to see his vision of a sandy beach through to fruition. Finally, satisfied with the beach, he left his shoes in the sand, tore off his shirt, and ran down the dock past my mom and sisters.

"Come on," he shouted and my sisters squealed. He dove in followed by Hannah and little Bess, just four years old. "Come on, Em," he called again.

I watched from my swing, miffed that he was swimming with my sisters and not swinging with me, as I had been the one waiting for him. I leaned back and let go and the swing took me out over the lily pad bay where leeches lurked and snapper turtles lived. I did not want to be part of the family games anymore or to carry the baby on my hip, clumped in a group with my sisters, all of us differing shades of blond as though we modeled one child at five stages of her growth.

"Em," he called one last time. I could see my mom looking up at me in question, as I let go again and sailed over the lake pretending not to hear my father. The part of me that still longed to run down to the lake and jump into my dad's arms was no longer strong enough to pull me away.

→>-<-

To a ten year old, a place of your own is sacred. At the top of the hill down the drive, but not out of sight from the cabin, stood a playhouse built by my father. It was a two-story structure with an A-frame roof and monkey bars off the back. Inside, an upturned crate made a stove on which stood an old metal teakettle for pretend boiling water. My father made a table of a round wheel of wood and cement blocks, upturned wooden boxes for seats. In the loft of the playhouse, I kept an old red lantern, its glass gone. I took that lantern with me the last time I visited the cabin before it was sold and destroyed. The lantern now sits in my bathroom with a paper heart hanging in place of the mantle.

I lay on my back in the loft of the playhouse staring at the white cocoons of armyworms. If I poked them with a stick they'd let out a small puff of musty air. Some years the armyworms invaded and demolished the leaves of the birch trees. When Hannah was a little girl, she fearlessly filled her shiny red purse with armyworms and brought it to show my mom, who laughed with admiration for her daughter's gift.

Alone, I stretched out on my back and crossed my legs at the ankle like I'd seen my father do. From the hill, Hannah called to me, but I ignored her. She would grow bored of looking for me and return to the dock and the beach, where our three little sisters and mom were spending the morning. I wanted only to be alone in this mysterious solitude—a first solitude, a longing to be separate and unseen. Silence opened up around me like a secret kingdom and what I would one day name reverence filled me in this moment.

I heard only the sound of the wind in the papery leaves of the birch trees and the intermittent song of birds. I smelled the wood and dust scent of the playhouse loft, immersed in forest, tucked away from the world. The ceiling was close enough for me to run a finger over its rough wood if I stretched out my arm.

When I finally climbed down from the loft no one called my name. My bare feet curled around each plank on the ladder. Outside I walked to the top of the hill. Alone, I was someone else, or truly me as my everybody-else-self slipped away. The birch trees, to a ten year old, looked like the city skyscrapers I had yet to see. I walked to the top of the hill. Hannah was digging in the sand on the beach with our sisters. Mom, with her golden hair and thin limbs, sat on a beach towel on the dock, the baby tucked under a makeshift shade.

𝆥 𝆥 𝆥 𝆥

I was not there (none of us were) when they tore down the cabin. I wonder if they removed the beautiful old sliding glass window before demolishing it. Did they leave the old wooden table and chairs inside? Did they haul out the loft beds to donate somewhere or were they beyond salvaging? Was there a small toy forgotten in a corner, discovered at the last minute, and dredged out for the children to play with? Has a little girl noticed the secret spot in the birch tree where she might store a note to her own mother as I did with mine? Or did they cut down the tree—tucked deep in the bark a final note left by my mom: *Meet me at the path to the woods after dinner. We'll go on a treasure walk.*

I now long to walk through the loft of the old cabin, drag my fingers along the rough wood of the ceiling beams, careful to avoid the sharp ends of nails, pounded through the thin roof. I want to lie on my parents' bed, level with the window, and look out at the lake and the island, to wake at the hollow edge of night to the cry of the loons. The water lapping against the shore, the Worshays' fishing boat out in the East Bay all morning, and the smell of heat in the grass, wind through the birch tree leaves triggering child-hood memories like firecrackers across the sky. I would only stay a little while, so as not to overdo it, become accustomed to the scents and sounds, emptying their ability to elicit memory should I en-counter them elsewhere.

Once while spending a rare weekend at the cabin when I was six-teen, my mom stood beside her bed in the loft, her back to me, spreading out the sheet. I walked up to fish a book out of my bag and find my swimsuit. She turned to me and said, "Sometimes, when I'm standing here, looking through the window at the dock and the lake, I forget where I am and it's like for a second I'm a young mom again with small children."

I know this feeling. We travel along the surface of time and then suddenly the layers give way and we are in another year, an-other body, another place. We've dipped down into a different layer on the geological map of life, and for a split second we re-ally are the other self again. It leaves so quickly that it might have never been, but the power of the instant lingers and we know we have been elsewhere.

⁂

That summer of my tenth year my father cut a path through the woods out to a point of land that looked over another bay of lily pads. Barefoot in my red swimsuit and shorts, I walked along the path listening for the sound of my sister close behind. But she was not there. It was just me tromping to the lily pad swamp. When I reached the end of the trail, I sat on a stump my dad had cut into a child's size chair and waited to see if I could spot the great blue heron my mom called Bed-Chuck Charlie. The lake was quiet and I could see a beaver dam at the back of the bay. I crept close to the edge of the water, searching its murky border. It frightened me that I couldn't see the bottom—lily pads of varying green covered the surface of the entire bay. Clumps of weeds floated on the lake

like water nests. I was poking the water with a stick, hoping to dis-
rupt a frog, when Charlie made his sweeping flight over the bay
and landed on the smooth egg-shaped rock along shore. *Charlie*,
I wanted to call. All animals, all things, had thoughts and spoke
to me at this age. Though the lake and the cabin lurked, living or-
ganisms of silence and solitude, they housed the mysteries of creature and child. *Charlie*, I held up my stick to him. But he stood stiff
and silent. In my mind, he was a hundred years old. I felt suddenly
lonely.

I longed for my sister then, as I turned back down the path. I
longed to find her, make her mine again. I ran through the woods
hoping she'd do spins with me on the gymnastics bar out behind
the playhouse or dive into the evening water, cutting open its thin
surface. I wanted to hear her voice, listen to her tell me a story or
command her to play a supporting role to my lead character. But
no one was in the cabin when I returned. How could they have left
me? I sat down on the couch and felt sorry for myself. There was
nothing delicious about involuntary solitude. It lacked the secret
pleasure of sneaking away, the relishing of the hidden self.

In my memory, the light began to fade as I sat alone in the cabin
feeling angry with my family, imagining they were out for ice
cream or down the road at Grandma and Grandpa's cabin visiting without me. But truly they had walked up the hill of the driveway to look for me and I wasn't alone for long. Soon, my mom
returned. We all went to visit our grandparents and cousins together. Still, in that moment of softening light, I sensed my small-
ness, all of my shimmering confidence slipped so easily away. I felt
how much I needed to be cared for, though the feelings I had then
didn't form such thoughts until much later, as the mind of time
writes meaning on the play of memory.

☙☙☙☙

The summer after my first year of college I frequently visited
the cabin alone or sometimes I'd bring a friend and light a bon-

fire beside the lake, drink whiskey until the stars blurred together into one body of shifting light. I was looking for the part of me that could not be recaptured, trying to put together a solid self or mourn the loss of childhood, which I did not yet realize would take a lifetime.

I move across the burgundy floor, perhaps I am sixteen, I am twenty-three, I am thirty. I stand in front of the built-in bookshelf and run my finger over its small selection. I look for the book *Love Story*, which I read in secret at the age of twelve, but it has long ago disappeared. On the wall beside the bookshelf hangs a photo of me in a plaid dress on the first day of second grade. Beside it hangs a photo of Hannah on her first day of kindergarten. Her hair is tied in a ribbon. She smiles the kind of humble smile that will forever be hers.

I realize I cannot let her go; I refuse to allow her to grow up. The memory of her as a child makes my chest tighten. Until a certain age she was so vulnerable: her hair always a mess, her clothes draped oddly across her slightly chubby body, a permanent Kool-Aid mustache on her lip. When I went away to college she refused to call me all that year as though I had abandoned her in leaving. She always spoke in silences. Then—it seemed suddenly—that little sister was gone. Her vulnerability zipped up inside, her body, a thin strip of itself, her hair parted and pared. Now, thirty-one to her twenty-nine, I still catch glimpses of her younger self: a loud outburst of anger, a wild love for games and competition, moments of complete abandon. When I see her, she sits on her outdoor patio beside Perch Lake, while her husband bakes bread in their wood-fired oven. She sips a glass of wine, entertains guests, and wears a chic black dress though it's covered in flour from baking. She gardens, paints the walls of her new home, puts up antique pictures of flowers that match the curtains. I am no longer useful, no longer a guide or a translator for her. I am her oldest sister, the sister that lives far away, and the one who forgets to call.

But in the picture from the cabin she remains that child, just as my gawky younger self, longing for a secret life, lived in those walls and woods, lake and sky. Parts of all of us remained there in memory. My mom always claimed her father's fingerprints were captured in the stain of the ceiling planks. I can remember her pointing them out to me as a child after her father had died in his sixties from cancer. His U.S. Navy cap hung from a hook on the wall at the cabin until we sold it. Now my mom keeps it in her bedroom along with other paraphernalia from the past. Amid the creamy whites and pastels, the old hat looks like a relic of another world—and it is.

These objects caught up in memory, hedged into the living world of the present, speak to me. What is this need to remember or demolish the past? We would not of course survive without the mind's endless capacity for storing memory. And yet the more I take out the memory of the past, like objects to be held and fondled in the present, the more those memories change, morph from the emotions of the present in which all things are kept. We are a people obsessed with our histories and some say it is because we want our lives to stretch out to the prehistoric past and into the future where those who follow us will be driven to dig for us, know who we were, remember. But I am partial to the idea that we simply want to feel connected to something larger than our single selves. So much of who we are took root in childhood, so we dive back into the maze of memory in order to understand. We seek the history of our people in hopes of finding clues in the DNA passed down like stories of who we are, who we're supposed to be.

In the silence and solace of my room now, I sit with these distant others. They do not pay much attention to me. A ten-year-old girl with thick blond hair cut short, with skinny legs, and a small body, looks over the jewelry scattered on the dresser top. She tries on a ring, but it slips from even her thumb. A young man with blond streaks in his brown hair is reading in the rocker, his legs crossed at the ankle; another likeness of this man hooks a worm on the end of a fishing line, "There you go. Now cast it," he's gently repeating. My young mother, her face always most beautiful in the morning, toasts bread in the gas oven at the cabin. And my sister in her blue swimsuit with the white ruffle sits on the edge of the bed swinging her legs, "Want to go swimming, Em?" And how I wish I could tell her yes, a hundred times.

It was years ago now that I last saw the cabin the summer before it was sold. While I was visiting my parents, my mom told me to go see it and say goodbye. I walked through all its rooms alone, stood in the loft beside the bed and looked through the window. The dock was lopsided and missing an entire section.

I don't think I lingered there for long. The visit felt unceremonious. In truth, everything I longed for of that place already existed in the reliquary of my memory. As I left, I walked up the hill from the lake, past the cabin, through the uncut grass that grew to my knees. I looked once more through the glass windows that reflected sky. I stopped at the top of the hill to look down. The breeze blew softly from the lake, through the leaves of the birch trees and the grass. Someone should collect all the sticks in the yard, I thought, so that Dad can mow when he gets here.

Ancestry of Illness

A week after my husband, son, and I arrive in Minnesota for the summer, I visit my grandparents' former home at 3001 Third Avenue East. It's a sleepy town with hardly much traffic, but as I pull up in front and park, I remember that Grandma banned us from crossing the street as kids. Dull butter-yellow-colored stucco with brown window trim, the house hasn't been painted in decades. It looks haggard and unloved but for a hanging plant in full bloom on the front stoop. My aunt and mom are selling the last of my grandma's belongings, and my aunt, unable to afford the place, will move into an apartment across town. As I lug baby Moses, three months old, in his car seat up the sidewalk and the steps to the front stoop, I wonder how many times I've walked through this door. How many lives have come and gone here? Our ancestry to this house is ending and with it all the nested past it might retain.

My aunt rushes toward me with a loud hello and oversized hug. "Emma-lee," she cries, and I hold tight to her. My mother scoops Moses out of his car seat and nestles him into the crook of her thin, sturdy arm. She has always been abnormally good at arm wrestling and now that I have a baby (she had six) I understand why: nearly everything is done with Moses on my hip held up by a single arm. My aunt and mother coo at Moses while I look around at the empty house. They're having an estate sale, but I'm not sure I want to see what they're selling. My aunt has already sorted through most of my grandmother's possessions, giving away jewelry and keepsakes to relatives, selling what she could online.

I see the old oak dresser that my mother helped Grandma pick out. It was after Grandpa died that my mother took her mother shopping for new bedroom furniture, insisting she spend the money on something nice for herself. It's priced ridiculously low at two hundred dollars. I run my index finger over the freshly Windex-cleaned mirror and consider buying it. I can picture this dresser in my grandmother's bedroom at the end of the hall, the one she occupied until my aunt moved her into the small bedroom at the top of the stairs. As a teenager, my grandma's house possessed infinite potential for discovery. I would open the top drawer of her bureau looking for the small white jewelry boxes from the Home Shopping Network that she always bought. Usually vibrant gemstones set in shiny yellow low-karat gold or silver. If I liked something, I would ask her about it, and if she hadn't already promised it to another granddaughter, she'd offer it to me. Sometimes I'd pocket one of the slim packs of gum left there for my sister Hannah, who liked chewing gum during basketball games. In her bathroom, I'd sniff face creams, dab a little on my cheek, and rub my arms with body lotion. In the kitchen, I'd search the cupboards for sweets or dig out an ice cream sandwich from the deep freezer. I'd drink the sweet iced tea or A&W Cream Soda she kept stocked in the fridge while I sat in front of the television watching game shows with her.

I watch as my mother bounces Moses in her lap. He is her first grandchild, though already a second has been born and another is due at the end of the summer. For a moment, I feel relief that my mother isn't the one with cancer. But that feeling turns quickly into guilt—life has always seemed harder for my aunt. My grandma had breast cancer twice. First at the age of fifty-nine and again at sixty-six. Each time she had a mastectomy and recovered. My mother says that because of this she developed the false perception that breast cancer was relatively curable. In some cases, it is, but not in my aunt's. Unlike my grandmother, my aunt has inflammatory breast cancer, which is particularly aggressive and rarely goes into remission. Most women don't survive with it for

more than a couple of years. It often feels like she was dealt an un-
fair hand in life, but she has a way of cultivating gratitude—a fire
garden in her midst—and a way of making the world her own.

In her early forties, she left her husband and drank herself half
to death. But after a monthlong inpatient treatment, she moved in
with her mom and quit drinking for good. It was her example of
early recovery that I would turn to when I realized I too carried
the family disease of alcoholism. Seeing her at this bottom—alcohol dependent, barely functional, locked in her bathroom drunk—
and then watching her dig herself out allowed me to imagine that
possibility for myself. For all her struggles, she was able to rise
above; always, she kept going, she pushed through. For a while,
she attended recovery meetings, read books about spirituality, and
seemed to follow that path. But, like most things in her life, she
eventually preferred to make her own way through sobriety and
quit attending meetings or even referring to herself as an alcoholic.

She went back to school and studied English literature around
the same time that I was in college studying the same subject,
drinking myself numb. We emailed each other often and I felt
drawn to her openness, sensed something shared between us
though I could not then say exactly what. She seemed happy despite the ongoing conflicts with her ex-husband over money and
their daughter. I felt her come alive in the poetry she wrote. She
offered me warmth and mutual understanding, a respect that few
adults had extended to me at the time. I offered her my admiration
for the work she did as a student and writer.

I find a pile of memorabilia—old slides, photographs, and papers.
I wonder if I can get the slides developed, but when I hold them
up to the light, I don't recognize the people in the photographs.
Trash, I think and toss them aside. I can't help resenting my aunt
for picking through everything, selling moneymakers online, including two Bob Dylan yearbooks that belonged to my grandfather, a teacher at Hibbing High School, where Dylan graduated.

Though she was probably swindled, they sold for several thousand each. She needs the money. Unable to work, she receives paltry disability checks and her ex-husband will not pay child support for their youngest daughter, who lives part-time with my aunt. Had she worked outside of the home and paid into social security, she would receive more, perhaps double, but she was a mother, a homemaker, and a wife—doing the unpaid work of women—and so she is forced to spend the last years of her life on the edge of poverty, with her family offering what help they can.

I am reminded of the Ray LaMontagne lyrics, "You beg, you steal, you borrow," in a song he wrote about a "young man, full of big plans and thinking about tomorrow." My aunt may have once been full of such plans, perhaps when she became a college student in her forties. It was then she came into her own, becoming a woman of intellectual prowess and creative brilliance, excited about nearly every subject she studied. She adored Shakespeare. But now her life feels picked apart and exposed as she is forced to beg, steal, and borrow to make a decent home for herself, a place her three daughters and grandchildren will take comfort in visiting much like we all felt when visiting Grandma.

When my aunt moved in with my grandma ten years ago, it was to get back on her feet, but then she stayed to take care of Grandma when her health started to decline. It was difficult and my aunt, who already struggled with depression, must have felt overwhelmed and isolated. She talked to her sister about it, trying to explain both the pain and frustration she felt. I can still hear my mother's hushed voice on a phone call with her sister, "Oh, Kris, I'm sorry you feel this way," and eventually, "what do you think we should do . . . I'm going to call about it tomorrow." But my aunt would change her mind out of guilt or fear, uncertain. In the morning, she'd see her mother again, remember her insistence that she never be put in a nursing home, and go soft. Everything is better in the morning. It would be okay for a while and then, just like the black dog of depression, her patience would wane, her sense of isolation would overwhelm her, and she would again feel trapped. Looking back on my own life, I see a similar pattern and can only imagine the sense of isolation my aunt must have felt at times, shouldering the weight of her mother's life day after day while she tried to get her own life off the ground.

Once she wrote a poem in which she talked about holding her mother's hand to cross the street and washing her piss-soaked sheets. The finality of their role reversal ignited anger in her, a pulsing fury like a heart on fire at the center of the house. But the poem revealed her understanding of life's dualisms—the anger with the love. She understood acutely that one never canceled the other. The truth that hurt could also heal when spoken, released into the artistry of well-placed words. We sent each other poems, written in secret and hidden away, poems that bore out the realms of our vulnerabilities and gave passage to our own survival. Poems we were afraid to share for fear of being misunderstood, judged, and belittled. Poems that spoke truth about what it means to be human, to struggle, to suffer and still find the gold, the light in it all, which my aunt did well.

After she got sick she started staying up at night sewing rather than writing. She quilts, makes clothing, and sews wall hangings for her children, grandchildren, and family. I think it's her way of living on into a future from which she will be absent. I imagine her working late on a winter night at the house on Third Avenue East, her fingers moving in a rhythmic dance over fabric, her cigarette going to ash in a clear glass ashtray already full. In the darkened kitchen, she stands at the sink looking out the window into the snowy street: a memory of childhood rises—her father pulling her on a sled—she smiles and feels the depth of her exhaustion. She fills her glass of water and goes upstairs to take her pills and fall asleep. The fire in her heart nursed to bed.

The house began to change when my aunt moved in with her youngest daughter. In a way, the house transformed in sync with my grandmother's decline. My aunt rearranged the furniture. New objects replaced the old steady ones that had been there for years, their constancy offering comfort to those who passed through. When she removed the mirror in the stairwell, I felt a slight devastation. I had spent my whole adolescence into young adulthood ambling down the stairs, getting a foot-by-foot glimpse of myself in that mirror. Its location seemed like a vital organ in the house or a necessary appendage. There was something so pleasing about seeing one's self a segment at a time—feet, calves, thighs, hips, belly, bust, neck, and face—and not all at once. Then the mirror over the mantel went missing.

My grandma's bedroom became the room at the top of the stairs, the one where I often spent Christmas Eve before we moved back to Minnesota permanently. The tiny TV at the foot of her bed was always turned on, though often muted. By then Grandma no longer smoked. Fearful she'd set the house on fire, my aunt convinced her that she had already quit. When I visited back then, Grandma said little, but patted my hand and smiled at me. She seemed content in that little room, her last before she was moved into a home that provided constant care.

My aunt gave us all the gift of my grandma securely in the comforts of her own home—it just wasn't quite her own home anymore. After my grandma died, when the house became my aunt's, by default, the carpets were torn out and the wood floors refinished. She painted the walls bold colors that Grandma would have said looked like either a "gallbladder attack" or an "upset stomach." I am comforted by these phrases as I walk through the red-walled living room, into the kitchen with the pea-green cabinets. My grandmother's coffee mug collection no longer hung on hooks covering the walls. Each cup had been distributed among her offspring, broken, or lost. Some turned up in my mother's kitchen.

In kinship with my aunt, I too rearrange the rooms in my apartment endlessly. Every spring I want to repaint the walls, switch out a bookcase for a chair, purchase a new rug, put up curtains, or take them down. On certain days when I am overwhelmed by anxiety, when I face a particularly daunting task, I push the furniture into the middle of the room and wash the walls and the floors with a bucket of soapy water, before I rearrange. Always, when I am done, I feel a sense of relief in the visual order I've created, the black dog appeased if only for today. I too have rooms painted gallbladder-attack pink and upset-stomach yellow, finding a certain joy in uncommon expression, in taking risks with paint shades, in making a space into my home.

Out on the back porch I find an old photograph of my mother and her younger brother. It's black and white but I think of my young mother's strawberry-blond hair. She was the second child in the line of four siblings, playing the role of the golden girl. She did well in school, became a cheerleader, graduated from college, and grew her hair long but became a born-again Christian with my father rather than a free-lovin' hippie like her big brother. My son's birthday is six days after my mother's. Their first year of life follows the same seasons from a winter birth. My mother's father tossed her into the air while standing in a lake, letting her little legs splash into the water just as I will toss my son this summer. He, like my mother as a baby, laughs and laughs. Looking at the photo I sense how quickly time passes, the body ages, and we are gone.

A photograph of my closest cousin and her mother, my aunt, falls loose from a stack. My cousin holds her baby in her arms—a beautiful boy. For a moment, I feel the familiar crush and panic of not knowing where she is or how to find her. I want to be ten years old again with her at my side running down a forest path or twenty-nine with her at the Caribou Coffee drive-thru, both of us sober, both of us grasping at hope, as close as we will ever be. But no longer sober, she doesn't stay in touch with me. I want to sit with my aunt discussing Shakespeare or Mary Oliver before her illness takes hold of her at the too-young age of forty-eight. I want to live in that foggy place of before until the pathos of the present becomes more tolerable. I let the picture fall back into the pile that smells faintly of mildew.

On the kitchen table sits the golden apple my grandfather received when he retired from teaching high school civics, two years before his death at the age of sixty-four to lung cancer that had already spread to his liver when he was diagnosed. All of us were there with him out at the Burnt Shanty cabin the day he died. I was a child, playing in the lake with my sisters and cousins. They called us in to say goodbye to his lifeless body, a thin corpse eaten through by cancer. I sat beside his best friend, Hysh, who patted my hand as he wept.

Only one interested buyer stops by the sale. She examines the oak dresser with its attached mirror but doesn't bite. It's priced too low, I think, creating suspicion. It won't sell anyway, and my aunt will give it to her middle daughter—fated to become a family heirloom. I like to think of that dresser as a link between the women in my family: my mother buying it with her mother, my aunt giving it to her daughter, my cousin perhaps gifting it to one of her own daughters someday. "I wanted my mother to have something nice after my dad had died," my mom once told me. "I urged her to spend the extra money on the oak bedroom set." Similarly, my aunt wanted to give her daughter something nice, something that might last. The piece was crafted the year my grandmother was born, 1922. How the objects in our life extend such meaning, I'll never know, but the history of our things gives joy. Somewhere in the year of 1922, a furniture maker cuts and fits the boards of this dresser as my grandmother enters the world. Often, I run my fingers over the seams of the baby blankets my aunt made for my son and think of how her own fingers followed that same seam as she sewed. I see her hands feeding the fabric under the gentle light of the machine.

My mom brews a pot of coffee in a coffee maker that by the looks of it will never again produce fresh anything, and the three of us sit at the kitchen table with our mugs while Moses sleeps. My aunt beams as she tells me about the little girl and her mother who bought the Barbie Dream House. "At first, I didn't think her mom was gonna go for it, but the little girl really loved it. I was so happy she got it." I smile as she tells the story, and I know my aunt will imagine, with a mixture of joy and nostalgia, that little girl playing with her new house.

Together, my aunt and mom are a duo that only makes sense to them, which is true of many sisters. My grandma often called Trish and Kris by the other's name, and the two of them would parody this at times. They insisted she demanded more from them, her two daughters, than her two sons. Within our family, they are known for their spontaneous singing and dancing performance of a song called "Sisters," by Irving Berlin, that perhaps they saw performed in the movie *White Christmas*, which came out in 1954, the year before my mother was born and six years before the birth of my aunt. Off-key and arms draped around each other, they'd croon while kicking up their legs in unison. "Sisters, sisters / There were never such devoted sisters," the song began. It always ended in laughter, but we girls—their daughters—loved it as kids. When my husband first experienced this song and dance routine, toned down over the years to a mere swaying with arms linked, he blushed with embarrassment. But they never cared. Laughter was of the gods to them.

Today we discuss the future of the house and my aunt's new life. I can tell she's proud of the updates she's made to the house. She sips her coffee and repeats the compliments some of her neighbors offered when they stopped by to browse the sale. "So many people thought the house was beautiful. I just know it's going to sell," she says. I nod, uncertain, and then the two of them are off imagining the nice young family they hope will make this house their home.

It will be the last time we do this here together, and later I will think of the decade's worth of coffee drunk at that table in that kitchen by women telling stories and offering each other the comfort of knowing laughter. When she came home from school as a child, my mother found lipstick stains left on the cups by her mother's friends from the neighborhood. She still imagines those

1960s mothers with painted smiles from which smoke coiled—
women of the greatest generation, whose husbands and brothers
fought in World War II and whose parents raised them during the
Depression era. I have always lingered in kitchens, drawn to the
warmth there, the place of women and the work that holds generations together in every family.

So much has passed through these rooms since my mother and
her sister were girls, and in a way, the transformed house makes it
easier to leave, as though it has already begun to morph into another home, another future with its own ancestry. Eventually, I
say goodbye. I walk out the front door for what I don't then realize will be the last time. Driving away from the house, my sadness
recedes as I begin to think of my son and my husband, the family I
am creating.

～ ～ ～ ～

Just after we arrive in Minnesota, Moses learns to roll over. He
rolls from back to belly and gets stuck there. He dislikes flopping
around on his belly and cries, and so I flip him back, but his urge
to roll overpowers him. He swings his legs up and throws his arm
down and turns again. I let him grunt a while on his belly until it
turns into a soft humming cry. When I pick him up he howls. I rub
my cheek against his and kiss it. Along with this new passion for
rolling, he begins cutting teeth, the first coming through a week
after we arrive. It all seems a fitting part of our transition to extended family life and a good way for him to keep me close.

Three weeks pass before I try to call my cousin. We know she's
in Duluth, but she hasn't kept in contact with any of us. She won't
answer my calls but responds to a text message I send her: "Just
soaking up the sun."

I write back, "Are we going to hang out?" trying to sound casual.

She counters with, "Of course."

But we never make plans. We have lived all these years tethered to each other with unbending resilience—sometimes in hate,
anger, or hurt, but mostly in love. We share the firstborn's cowl
of inner fury that seems a special gift of the Arnason blood, along
with the family disease of alcoholism. I admit that I have resented
her at times for her absence, but right now I long for her. For the
past year she's fallen away again, and for the first time in her life
she has lost her son, now a teenager, to her disease. He refuses to
speak to her and lives instead with her father, his grandpa. And
I, for the first time in my life, understand what it means to have a
son. But I want her here with me and I'm angry she won't quit.

Alcoholism is a disease of lies. Your lies, they say, will kill you.
Akin to depression, it's a disease of the mind that wants to kill you
and thus you have to stay in recovery, you have to maintain healing, as the disease never fully leaves you. Nobody seems to understand this in my family and I have quit attempting to explain, let
them believe it's about drinking and using. Let them believe one
can just stop and be okay. It's exhausting.

My grandfather seemingly got away with only an early and
rather unpleasant death, while keeping intact his family, home, career, and never landing himself in a jail or an institution. But what
do I really know about his life? How many years did he spend
passing out in that La-Z-Boy? What did he do with the grief of
his past, a past that included entering the navy at the tender age of
seventeen, in the midst of a war, where he collected the remains of
the dead? I don't know what ghosts followed him, but I can tell by
the way alcoholism has infused my family that it had its claws in
deep.

It is a disease of denial, not just for the alcoholic. My mother
tells me that her father loved life, loved his family, and loved people, which might have been true. But she seems to have worn
blinders through her youth and never quite let herself absorb the
dark side of his disease, just as she has never completely understood the depth of mine.

My grandfather's oldest son, also an alcoholic, did not get away with as much. As a child, I adored him. He put me on his shoulders and sang to me, bought me gifts like a birdfeeder, and gave me cards made of birch bark. I still remember the house (an old fixer-upper) my uncle owned with his partner, who didn't shave her body and let her dark hair grow long. There was a picture of her brother in a frame on the wall. He'd died young on a dare, holding onto a lift bridge as it rose. She birthed their three children at home. It seemed a happy life and one that intrigued me at a young age. Perhaps I was already drawn to a bohemianism that might allow for excessive binge drinking and recreational drug use in the name of love and freedom. But probably it had more to do with their tender openness. I felt welcomed and respected, an equal, which is not something I felt among most grown-ups.

Alcohol eventually got the better half of both of them and they split up. Sometimes my uncle is sober. My mother told me that he recently held his first grandbaby hours after she was born. Nestled in his arms, she slept while her proud grandpa rocked her. But he has never stayed sober for long, and why should I be surprised—the statistics around alcoholism and recovery are dire. Most of us live out our lives in misery, and I may return to that destiny.

True, my particular creed believes that pain is the touchstone of spiritual growth—we discover who we are through struggle. But mostly I believe because I could not otherwise bear the impermanence of this life and the suffering of attachment. Watching the diseases of cancer and alcoholism tornado through the lives of those I love as well as my own has brought me close to the rage of disbelief. Though, just as quickly as anger pulverizes me, I am drawn back up into faith in a power greater than me, in a God whom I can barely fathom. The powerlessness of my own small life remains the central force, the heart, of this faith. "Stay humble," I whisper to myself some days. "Stay here." I think of my aunt, then, and how closely she lives to each day, spending nearly every summer of her life at the Burnt Shanty Lake cabin in the birch tree forest at the end of her "powdered sugar roads" that wind her there year after year. How she lay in the dark at the end of the dock with her youngest daughter, watching the stars, or dove off the end of the dock after running down the hill from the sauna, swimming out underwater forever, her body half fish. I remember how she crawled through the long grass in the neighbor's field at the cabin, playing lions and tigers and bears with us as little kids—her love fierce, like a wildfire in her heart.

❧ ❧ ❧ ❧

My grandparents' house was beautiful to me as a child who lived in apartments and a walkout basement until the age of fourteen. It was the place I returned to for holidays and celebrations. Warmth filled the kitchen where my grandmother baked pies for Thanksgiving and caramel rolls on Christmas morning, and where my aunt and mother hustled to get everything done for a holiday dinner. The Christmas tree shimmered with tinsel in the living room window, filled with candy canes we liked to sneak and eat upstairs in the bedroom my cousins, sisters, and I called the "pink room." The school photographs of every grandchild hung on the wall of the stairwell. Behind the current year's photograph of each child, there was a stack of photographs leading back to kindergarten. Each year revealed a slight change in the face of the child: her hair grown out or cut away, the spaces of missing teeth filled in with big ones.

I can still feel under my hand the brown marble-patterned carpet that covered the living room and dining room; I know the way my finger traced the inroads of that carpet as a child, imagining streets by which tiny toy cars might travel. I can smell the scent of the window glass (musty, distant), my nose pressed to it, in the bedroom at the top of the stairs, where I often slept during visits as a child. I see the snow-covered streets of Christmas through the window of that room. The streetlights close and warm. And when I remember that room, I feel the quickening of anticipation for morning that pulsed through me as I lay in bed with my sisters on Christmas Eve. From here, I am with my father standing before a new easel that I received from Santa. "Daddy, you draw," I say. But he giggles and tells me that he can't draw, he can only make stick people. I am the artist of the family, the drawer, although some of my sisters will also learn to draw and paint, and eventually I will give this art up altogether, choosing instead to record my secrets in writing. I am the keeper of the family secrets and the guardian to the lost.

Every room had a particular feel to it when my grandmother was still alive. In my grandparents' bedroom, to the left of the stairs, I imagine my grandfather's dress shirts filling the closet. I remember standing beneath them as a little girl, breathing in the faint scent of him—cigarette smoke and shaving cream from a red-and-white-striped bottle—the long sleeves with their buttons grazing my nose and cheeks. Though I wasn't there, I see my grandmother taking them out, throwing them down on the bed, weeks after her husband died, and deciding to get rid of them all, as though she might purge herself of the pain.

The red flower-print wallpaper of the TV room, where my grandfather spent most of his time, was once my mother and aunt's bedroom. As girls, after they were tucked in for the night, they waited for the beams from passing cars to flash across their wall, sometimes playing a game to see who could touch the light first. When it was the TV room, a framed picture hung on the wall of a wolf standing on a snowy ledge overlooking a small prairie home. Grandpa said the print often hung over the fireplaces of the farmhouses in North Dakota where he had grown up. The blue La-Z-Boy where my grandfather spent most of his spare time was covered in cigarette burns. He often fell asleep watching TV, smoking and drinking cans of beer or tomato juice. In the morning, I'd find him stretched out on the sofa under an afghan, most likely crocheted by Grandma. I wonder if he dreamed of that prairie in North Dakota, of the wolves of his youth, or of the war. I wonder if he too loved this old house.

But like the evolution of the house, as I've grown older, my mother's family erodes. Year by year the cracks appear: an irreparable brokenness between certain family members, a distance softened only by the memories of time we spent with each other—our childhood like a misty fairy tale that we might have only dreamed. Death and disease break us down, whittle away at the bonds we've maintained, until they're cut too thin.

Mostly I see it as the slow demise of an alcoholic family, within which no one is left untouched, everyone must seek her own redemption, her own salvation. We're not without our redeeming qualities, but might not the maternal half of my family better off exist in the reliquary of nostalgia: relics of a former life where poverty, disease, addiction, and self-destruction still lay dormant within?

In truth, they are most beloved by me and most longed for as they are, rife with loss and the incurable sorrow of addiction.

☜ ☜ ☞ ☞

Josh and I walk along the dirt road from my parents' house with the baby nestled in a sling around my shoulder. Moses stares up at the trees that hang over the road of my parents' quarter-mile-long driveway. I grab Josh's hand and squeeze it, feeling the warmth of his skin. We have been here a month and we'll stay another month before returning to Vermont, where he'll start his first year as a kindergarten teacher.

"I don't want to die," I say as though for the first time.

"Cancer kills us all," Josh blurts out. "That's what we die of now, in our era."

He senses my attunement to my aunt and the way her illness occupies my daily thoughts here. Yet he's right, in a way, though heart disease remains the leading cause of death in the United States. Josh thinks I have an abnormal fear of death. Not just since the baby, but since he's known me. Some nights, back when we were living together in a studio apartment with robin's-egg-blue-painted walls, I'd wake and beg him to promise that he would come find me if he died first. "Okay, okay," he'd mumble and fall back to sleep. He does not think often of death. He calls death a new beginning. Though I'm the one who believes in God. I tell him he's in denial and he shrugs—a shrug that comforts me as though releasing me from the talons of my fear, brushing death off his shoulder for now.

The nature of cancer terrifies. It's unpredictable, devious, and unruly. Some forms of cancer are easily arrested and removed, while others seem to kill with fierce determination. New types are constantly appearing. It's hard not to characterize cancer as vengeful, call it cruel, and pretend we can fight it out of us—our body, our home. When my aunt was diagnosed, we did not know what course it would take, but we knew it was terminal and fatal. So far, while it has dashed her hopes for the future she imagined, she continues to live a life that's somewhat manageable. She tells my mother that she doesn't want to be known as a cancer patient, doesn't want to attend support groups for cancer survivors just as she doesn't want to attend groups for alcoholics. She does not want her disease to become her identity.

"Cancer becomes a disease of shame, one that encourages secrets and lies, to protect as well as conceal," writes Terry Tempest Williams. I startle at the word "shame." It's true that when we hear that someone has cancer, self-fear often overwhelms our compassion. Will I be next? Will my beloved, my child? With cancer, the body turns on itself and begins a process of self-destruction. Does the body grow to hate its home, just as the alcoholic and addict grows to hate herself, to fear what she will do?

We are surrounded by a cancer industry that sells us the idea that we as individuals are capable of inoculating ourselves from cancer by consumption of super foods or tonics or by avoiding certain toxins. Why didn't you quit smoking? Why didn't you eat healthier foods, run miles, do yoga, learn to grieve properly for the death of your mother, your father, your daughter? Just as those unfamiliar with the disease of alcoholism and addiction seem to blame the user—why can't she just stop, she's ruining her life? In reality, we are powerless.

Days after our walk, Josh texts me a quote purported to be from Chief Seattle's speech of 1855, which Josh came across in a book he was reading while working at the hardware store in the basement of the pharmacy my father owns: "There is no death, only a change of worlds." Just as there are manifold changes of worlds within this life.

My aunt once told me that as a little girl staying at her paternal grandma's house in Grand Forks, North Dakota, she woke in the middle of the night and walked out into the hallway to find her grandmother, a first-generation American from Iceland, standing buck naked in the middle of the kitchen drinking from a bottle of vodka. In my mind, I see her long white hair draped over her back, her breasts hanging loose off her ribcage. I know this is not likely true and that my version of the story has morphed into a myth of a wild woman, my great-grandmother, but it comforts me. I want to connect the dots between generations of alcoholics, to point a finger at the disease. Grandma Sigrid lost her two sisters when they were young women and later her husband, Charles, and their youngest son died in a small craft airplane accident when my grandpa was forty years old.

At the moving sale, my aunt's hair was short and gray. Her face has curled into the face of history, of time, and of her Icelandic ancestors who traveled from northern Iceland through Canada and into North Dakota four generations ago. They were people who suffered through disease and death of their own, so that they might live a better life. My aunt looks young despite her gray hair. But in her face, I read things—lines like the inroads of the old carpet I played on weave a story. I sense pain and betrayal. Does she feel betrayed by the world, cheated out of life? I see determination there too, and hope. She doesn't know when she will die, but she knows how and that it will occur sooner than she had expected. Every day she quietly copes with the pain of her disease while facing the unpredictable course of her future. She once told my mother, her only sister, "I'm not lucky, but I'm blessed." I think she knew this all her life.

⋙ ⋙ ⋘ ⋘

A few weeks after the estate sale at my grandma's, I find a photograph of my cousin tacked to an old bulletin board in my childhood bedroom, now the room I share with my son and husband. I carefully lift the tack and take the picture. We are young, early twenties, and I can see youth in our eyes—still so clear and undaunted by time and life. The skin of our cheeks, rosy and fresh, flaunts the beauty of youth, something we took for granted. She was so beautiful, I think. We were beautiful.

I always thought my cousin would be there when I had my first child. We grew up raising her son. She found out she was pregnant at fifteen and called to tell me on a hot day in August. We hadn't talked in months, which wasn't unusual back then. Regardless of the time between us, we easily reconnected when we sought each other out again. I was wearing a yellow bikini with tiny flowers embroidered on it that day she called. I sat on the edge of the dock with the cordless phone, my feet in the water. My parents weren't around.

"What are you going to do?" I asked.

"Have a baby, I guess."

"Really?"

It was hard for me to imagine this and it definitely sounded like a bad idea to me. In truth, she was the only one in her life who wanted the baby. Everyone else, including our grandma, advised her against keeping the pregnancy. But she insisted as though she knew he would be her greatest joy, and she was right.

At the time, she was as wild as ever, but once her son was born she became a different person. She stayed sober for years on her own, living with her parents until she finished high school and then moving into an apartment with her son while putting herself through community college. When their father remarried, she took in one of her sisters and cared for her while she struggled to find her way. Her door was always open to my sisters and me then, no matter what we were going through. She was a gentle mother and it was clear that she loved her son fiercely.

I slide the picture of us over the glass of a framed black-and-white photograph of our grandma as a small girl standing at the edge of a North Dakota prairie. It sits there on the desk, a talisman of hope.

⁂

My grandparents, a schoolteacher and a nurse, bought the house on a corner lot with pride, eager to raise their young family. In slides from the sixties, they stand in front of the house with their happy family, looking toward a certain future. The slides flicker to reveal my stylish and slim grandma smoking a cigarette, my long-haired uncle tossing a football, my other uncle reading a book, my aunt proudly holding up a fish she caught with her dad, and my mom as a spunky long-haired girl doing cartwheels.

Then I am two years old running up the stairs the day my first sister, Hannah, was born, calling, "The baby's coming, the baby's coming." I jump onto my grandparents' bed—they still share a bed—and topple into their waiting laps. I am sitting in the living room, the sheer curtain always drawn, holding my second sister, Alida, the day she came home from the hospital. My grandma and I have decorated a cake with sugarcoated gumdrops. My grandpa sits at the head of the kitchen table correcting civics papers with a two-sided blue- and red-ink pen, a writing utensil that fascinated me as a child. I smell Grandma's caramel rolls on cold mornings in winter. I taste sweet iced tea on hot summer afternoons. I hear the spoon clank in the glass as she stirs it and the ice cubes cracking from the tray. I will not return again, and the house will fall to memory, to the unguarded parish of nostalgia, but the myth and story of it remains growing stronger with every year. In Korean, the word for *house* is the same as for *home*; there is no way to differentiate. To sell a house, then, carries with it a deeper sense of loss.

Home, at my parents', I lie close to my son as he falls asleep between Josh and me. Sometimes I wrap my body around him like a shell. He breathes into me. My body—his former home—comforts him. I watch him sleep. As his mother, I find him alarmingly beautiful. The lines of his face have a pleasure to them, and when I wake some mornings and see him sleeping beside me, curled into me with one little hand outstretched to rest on my arm, I am crushed by the enormity of my love for him. I sense the potential devastation of my attachment to him but it does not stop me.

My aunt has moved into an apartment near one of her closest friends. Her walls are freshly painted, the objects of her life arranged and ordered. I imagine her with her coffee in the morning, her heart light with gratitude for fresh starts, new homes, and the gift of an ordinary day. In the living room at my parents' home, my mother sits with baby Moses while he rolls over again and again. Josh strums his guitar beside me on the couch. He winks at me. I feel lucky. Moses cries and my mom picks him up and places him on his back again. Immediately he rolls over. It's exhausting just to watch him do it. But I marvel at his determination. The sheer force of his will not yet fixed to any one place, to time and history, but of his body, an ocean yet bound, a home unto himself.

Self-Portrait

Young Woman Drinking

Mother should have told me that booze made a kind of heaven in my body, I thought the first time I felt it. I was fourteen and shared a six-pack of 3.2 beers from a gas station with a girl named Edie who, like me, would become an alcoholic. It was fall, new school feeling, shoes still clean and hair smelling of chlorine from diving practice in the pool. We walked to an old brick apartment building across the street from the gas station. Our town was small, a population of less than five thousand. We climbed the dimly lit stairs to the second floor and knocked on the door. I remember thinking the building was old, and feeling a pleasure in its age along with the loose nerves of my body, the fire of anticipation.

Man in a Room

Edie knew a man. She'd gotten him to buy for her before. I don't recall paying him more than the few dollars required for the beer. We knocked and a tall American Indian man with pockmarked skin, a red nose, and a ponytail came to the door. It was impossible to tell his age—old, I guess I would have said then, but probably no more than forty-five. The room was clean and sparse. We sat on a couch made of stiff and scratchy upholstery I would later encounter in a chair I was given for my first college apartment. The man nodded to us as we went in. He kept his distance and didn't look at me directly. I remember feeling safe, believing he would not harm me, though I cannot say if this instinct was well developed in me, a girl who had spent her life until then in the safety of privilege. It was likely my naivete that led to feelings of safety and from which the daredevil in me would soon launch.

Meditation on Pretty

In the ninth grade, I became pretty. Men and boys began to look at me in a way that felt exciting and shameful. "Be careful," my father said, bewildered by fear, "men are dogs." I was still a child, what could I do? A girl who had lived powerless but for imagination and games.

"Look away," my father said when we passed men in a city shouting catcalls. But I looked them in the eye, and years later, drunk, I laughed. The man who twisted my nipple in a bar on spring break, the man on a train masturbating, the men in Italy hissing or stepping into allies to expose themselves to me, the American soldier in Spain who asked me to let down my blond hair—of course I did—the teacher wanting things, the boss fondling. But I'm lucky, right? Nothing really bad ever happened to me.

Two Girls on a Sofa

Edie and I sat on the rough couch in the small, smoky living room while the man went across the street to get our beer. Had I not gotten drunk for the first time that night, there would have been another night. I haven't thought much of this night until now, only that it rings symbolic or at least ironic in that Edie and I were simply two young women with a disease hidden in our bodies. Still, it was this very day in fall, with this girl, that I first found relief from my anxious mind. The world I had long imagined, the one in which I spoke to boys and laughed at parties and went to dances, came alive.

Woman on the Edge of a Bed

I don't know how long Edie and I sat on that couch looking at
the dead screen of an old TV before I realized that to my right,
through an open bedroom door, a woman was sitting with her
back to us on the edge of a bed. Behind her a sheer curtain veiled
the window through which light came in and made the edges of
her sharper. Dark braided hair and a heavyset build. I want to say
she whispered something, muttered or grumbled, but I don't really
know. I never saw her face. She never turned around. I want to remember it as if she were praying, but this isn't likely.

Rounded like a stone in a river, she did not move. She sat waiting for us to leave—perhaps afraid her friend would get in trouble,
but probably just annoyed. I watched the dust particles floating in
the shaft of light coming from the window behind the faux-wood-
framed TV. I had always thought it fascinating to be able to see
those little spots floating in the air, like magic. Edie and I did not
speak while we waited for the man to return.

I see only the rough edges of this memory but there was something about this moment, something spirited or anointed as though
a standing still occurred—time blipped, broke open to reveal my
fate, though only now through the tunnel of time and memory do
I see this.

Self-Portrait in Red

Nothing bad ever happened to me, I say, again and again, though
some days I'm not sure. I was born like this—jittery, sensitive,
anxious, and longing for relief—though I never knew I needed relief until relief came.

I became pretty and then angry and what do women do with
their anger? Where does a woman put her rage?

Woman at a Desk in a Pink Room

Sometimes I believe I have lived a thousand lives. This comforts me. *You have been here before, you will be here again. All the world is of this one breath.* And yet it is this very connectedness that allows for the unique experience of each one, allows us to divide and disperse like sharp points of light blow free. Even now at my desk in the pink room, with the sound of the city I live in drifting through my bedroom window, I can feel this connection. But what is holy, sacred, and beloved does not easily make itself known on the page. So I turn away from it. I know too, that day with Edie, more than twenty years ago now, was just another day, except that for me drinking would nearly destroy my life and this was the day I became smitten by its escape.

Girl in a Pretty Dress

I was still a child in the ninth grade when I became pretty, relatively safe, living in privilege in white America. I did not yet understand dehumanization or misogyny, that one makes the other an object in order to do things inhumane to her without guilt or conscience. I did not understand how men rape a woman, each taking a turn like a pinball machine. How one's pleasure can be thus, I will never know. How the threat of rape keeps women imprisoned, a kind of war against her body all her life. Each time I hear a report in the news, another piece of me goes numb, turns blue-black with death. Each time a man values a woman for her appearance, I remember how the scales balance on a spectrum that lighthearted jokes uphold. Knowing this, I stop myself from telling my niece her dress is "so pretty." Pretty is nothing but an ugly attachment to self-destruction, to seeing one's self divided—not as I am but as I am seen.

Self-Portrait in Red 2

Tell me, what does a woman do with her anger, with her rage, or with her shame over being made subservient, secondary, object? Where in her body does it live? How many times can she circle back?

John Berger writes, "A woman must continually watch herself. She is almost continually accompanied by her own image of herself." She sees herself through the eyes of a man looking at her looking at him, a self divided. What she cannot tolerate about the world she buries there, in her body.

Two Girls Walking Down Hill

The man returned and handed us our paper bag. Did we thank him? Did the woman scold him as we departed, taking the steps quickly, giddy, and eager? Looking back, I am certain that this man also carried the same disease and was a harbinger of what was to come for me. But, of course, I could not see this.

Edie and I walked slowly down the hill to her mother's blue house in the fading light of autumn. Edie may have promised good things to come or discussed the bad taste of our beers and how to alleviate this; I don't recall anything but the nervous anticipation I would often feel again in moments when I knew I would soon be drinking. Later on, my body would fill with calm in anticipation of the relief of alcohol.

I would see that man again, though I doubt he recognized me, when I worked the register at my father's drug store, which I did for many summers. I would see him waiting, stinking of cigarette smoke, hunch shouldered, and quiet, and I would wonder and want to know if he still lived in that apartment. And where was the stone-shouldered woman? He radiated a sorrow that drew me to him, perhaps it was intrigue or projection, but perhaps a part of me could already identify with his grief.

Self-Portrait with Bed

Even now, years into recovery, this disease rips apart my carefully stitched seams on certain days. I lie in bed and feel my body riveted by fear. There is no light in the sky, the window is close but I see only gray and the cracking arms of bare trees across the rectangle of lightlessness. I cry all day filled with relentless self-hatred: I am not good enough, I am failing at everything, I will never be enough. It is, some say, a disease of perception, for just yesterday I felt the warm heat of love, the light rabbit of creativity at my feet, the glow of children messing the house, tumbling about, wild with laughter, and the body of my husband like a luminous constellation at my back. I will feel it again if I go and sit with the others and tell them everything. They will nod and say, "Yes, us too, you are not alone." The opposite of addiction is connection. We will trade comforts like Sunday morning wafers on my girlhood tongue that I washed down with a thimble full of grape juice, sitting in a pew with my family. We will say, come back or you will die, speak the truth or you will die, and this will be true.

Self-Portrait of Arrival

When I felt drunk that first night, after gulping down three foamy, watery, bad-tasting beers, I thought of my mother. It was a fleeting thought in my mind but there it was: Why had she not told me about this? Why had she kept this ecstasy from me? All my life I had lived in a body riddled by nerves, tense, painfully shy in certain moments, acutely aware of the emotions of others, burdened by a longing to run free of it all. Everything would be okay now, I thought, if I could keep drinking on my way to drunk and never run out of more. Though there could never be enough.

This is it, I thought, as my body went numb with the most spectacular relief I had ever known, *I have arrived.*

The Blue Room

I arrive at a small apartment room in the basement of a cold winter. It is here my disease reaches its first pinnacle; it is here I spend entire days reading Eliot's *Four Quartets*. Alone, I could drink as much as I wanted. I could smoke and throw up in the trash bin, piss in it if I wanted. I made no friends in that city; I barely spoke to my roommates. I'd walk to class up a hill through the snow. In the spring, the first unbearable buds of green breached winter's gray distance. I recited Eliot to the wind that rattled my cheeks, burned my eyes, stung my young skin.

A part of me still lives there in that city by the lake with its foghorns howling through the amber night, its cold lake water lapping the stone shore, and the room. Every room I have lived in weaves its way through this room, as this room will become the color of the next, until the final rooms of a home outlive all the rooms of the past. Still, in the shadows, I will see the little Mexican ashtray overflowing, feel the carpet I scrubbed clean beneath my feet, smell the scent of air freshener mixed with stale cigarette smoke, of the cold winter basement room where I found Eliot as I began to lose myself.

Truth keeps in the rhythms of the body, the echo of a voice in your own, the pulse that rises sacred from the chorus, a brilliance. Year after year I lost and found Eliot just as I lost and found my addiction—forces of life always right there below the surface of the breath, at the bottom of the lungs, hollowing and hallowed. It was the measure of *Four Quartets*, when Eliot returned, that opened me. That turned a bird into a shredded glimpse of eternity, a city into a maze of destinies. Though I'd memorized the lines I loved best, the words were secondary. First the tempo, the cadence, then *quick now, here, now always*—

Before you tell a story, you sense its truth. Why then can you not explain the way the sparrow in the yard, as you hung the wet linens, broke your heart?

Josh came into the café where I worked Sunday mornings and ordered a small, black coffee. He sat alone and wrote in a journal. Once, I watched him tapping his foot on the floor, bending over a little notebook scribbling, and decided he was odd. It was winter. His beard was overgrown. His hair, uncombed and slick in certain places, knotted at the crown where he must have twisted around in his sleep. Later, I could imagine him doing that, wiggling around in his sleep, sprawling his legs before curling them up. I only noticed him for a minute before I went back to French pressing coffee and steaming lattes. This was back when he was still a sleepy woodsman type, a little bit of childish mischief playing around his furry lips. It's been so long since I remember him like that: happy, carefree, silly. In the end, he never laughed.

Josh was afraid to jump in the creek the first time he took me to the camp in the mountains of Vermont. The June humidity greased his skin while his long hair stuck to his neck. I wore my bathing suit under a yellow sundress I'd bought at a yard sale. My windswept hair looked like a lion's mane. Back then, I thought of myself as a lion. We sat on the rocks beside the creek, drinking warm cans of Budweiser and smoking rolled cigarettes. Josh didn't actually smoke tobacco, but he started when he met me because I didn't like marijuana smoking, which he adored. But really, he loved weed in the same way I loved booze.

The creek was up and fast from a wet spring and snowy winter. Josh dipped his foot in. I laughed and yelled at him, "Josh, you chickenshit!" I stood up and tore off my dress. In two steps, I'd leapt over the edge of the rock and plunged in. I swam like an eel, hungry for water. Hungry for everything; nothing was ever going to be enough.

Josh thought I was tough as nails, a sort of hard-ass feminist woman who wasn't taking any shit. I had nothing to lose, and I wanted to make sure you knew it. That was, of course, the last thing I was. I'd get drunk, tell him to fuck off, tell him he was weak and cowardly, that he'd end up a miserable old man. Josh went on loving me anyway, I guess, at least for a time. Sometimes I think of him then as courageous for loving me—but it wasn't courage.

To understand you have to understand that we are never going anywhere but where we've always been.

Today I lie watching clouds out the window from my sofa. They are something to me now . . . this movement through intangible space, the breaking and dividing and reconnecting. I watch and feel split down the middle, splayed and sliced. You belong to me, I think. Then: clouds move under the spin of earth, breached where white-blue easy cotton tears apart and the sun shimmers along the hems like something holy. It's June, new green leaves. His birthday arrives and passes. I saw the old typewriter collecting dust on the porch of his new place as I stood knocking. Nobody answered. I gave him that. Children ride bikes with helmets on their heads past the window where I watch the clouds. I saw Josh yesterday standing in the soft rain after a storm; he was smoking outside a bar. The sky held a gold haze and a rainbow that everyone came into the street to see. I said hello and asked him how he was doing, but I just kept walking as he shouted out, "Okay!"

The sun makes the edges of objects gleam: a jar full of seashells, the legs of the rocking chair, a candle on the coffee table burned to the wick. I am listening to Tom Petty for the first time in years. It reminds me of the way Josh doesn't know who he is and also the way he kissed my head and let my hair spill through his fingers.

Josh still talks about the trip to Nova Scotia as if it were our honeymoon, though half the time we felt wrecked by a distant emptiness. Smoke from the campfire where we cooked hotdogs, only yards from the sea, stung my eyes as I filled myself with cheap Canadian beer. Still, I loved that trip in a way, even driving the awful silver Mustang the guy at Avis offered us as a free upgrade as though bestowing a grand prize. He did not realize the extent of our bohemian snobbery, but we took it for the iPod connector.

We were changed, weren't we? Josh had an affair while I was away in Siberia and Mongolia for a month. He said, "I just didn't feel connected to you." I returned from thirty-six hours of traveling and we made love, and then, hours later at a restaurant, he told me he didn't think we were good together. I gulped down my beer and left him there. Returning home, I slept for days. Months passed before he told me that he'd had the affair. I could tell he was high, or maybe he'd said, "Shit, I'm really high." I was visiting my family in Minnesota, and having drunk too much, I called him and started interrogating him about other women. He said, "Well, actually," and my chest filled with the heat of rage.

We thought Nova Scotia could heal us. But we didn't know what was broken. On the beach, Josh handed me a piece of sea glass and I said, "It's sea glass." It was as if he felt stupid for not knowing the name or as if I'd ruined his treasure in naming it, but that wasn't it, of course. He ran down the beach away from me, flailing his limbs like a sea gull. I ran after him, in a moment of chivalry, and caught him by the arm: *Look, I know you don't know what to say . . . how to act.* But I didn't either. We stood there, turned to the ocean. I traced the horizon with my eyes, thinking of our first trip to the ocean in Maine. We read Hemingway aloud to each other, *The Garden of Eden.*

At Meat Cove, we camped on a hill overlooking the ocean and spent the afternoon sea kayaking in the fog. Josh paddled ahead of me. I watched his arms propelling the little boat forward and imagined a ballet of arms. Art, I thought, is less painful. He waited for me and we drifted side by side, together for a moment, silenced.

In Halifax, he gave up and said: I'm not enough for you. I should have said, *Of course not, nothing is*, but he had risked something and it humbled me. We made love on the bleach-scented sheets then ran out into the night to eat and eat and drink and drink until we could barely walk ourselves home.

I never knew what Josh wanted me to be, how he wanted me to be. I assumed he wanted me some other way because I did not want him the way he was. But, of course, such desires have only to do with one's own self-loathing.

If you see these words in linear time, they make no sense, but if you step beyond time into the melody of consciousness, truth may come.

When you lose your love you become estranged from your own body. Your body feels alien and unlovely. You want it to shrink or grow into another shape. A shape the old love will no longer recognize. His hands as they moved over the puzzling contours of this strange new country would go cold with the mystery of it.

I think of his body growing in my absence. It grows so large that it spills over the edge of the bed as I curl tight in the corner, hugging the bear my father sent me for Valentine's Day.

I shrank my body as best I could. Perhaps someone would feel sorry for me if I became too thin. They would say, "Look, what he's done to her!" But instead, of course, everyone complimented the slimmer me, so I went on smoking cigarettes and not eating, feeling sorry for myself.

Will it storm again tonight? If I smoke another cigarette will I throw up? Why does this neighborhood smell of grilled meat? Someone lights a firecracker and three dogs start howling. People here tie up dogs in the yard or the alley. Dogs on a rope tied to a tree howl, slobber, and bark until someone opens a window to scream. Where will I be? How will I arrive there? Will I ever stop longing?

I learn to listen to music again. I play all my old albums trying to understand what the voices want me to know. I lie on the sofa listening, while my pain morphs into rage and then back into pain again. It is either/or: pain or rage. I hate Josh. The hate makes me feel unclean. I love Josh and I feel pathetic. There is no salvation in loving someone like a dog. It feels like that to me, dog love.

Today I wake up loathing Josh. In the moment, each morning between dreaming and waking, I forget. But then I remember. Mostly, I remember everything. Though there are dark holes of drunk that have no memory. I go downtown wearing my swimsuit under shorts and a T-shirt that says, "I want you naked." (Who am I?) I wear enormous tortoiseshell sunglasses that cover most of my face.

He walks up before I notice him and says, "Why the long face?"

"Hi," I say.

"I just saw you," he says and sits down cautiously, "you were in my dreams this morning."

I want to roll my eyes, but instead I smile.

There is a period of regression between two broken lovers when they still act like lovers. They try to find new ways to kiss and hug, to touch an arm or a knee, but it always feels like old times for a while. The body moves of its own volition. If the old love is in the vicinity, the body senses this familiar comfort and finds it. Josh and I ran into each other almost daily. We lived in a small town, but still, I made efforts to avoid him that never seemed to work. But then, if I wanted to see him, felt some need to, he wouldn't be around.

Josh was nervous and shaky. Open, I thought. Sometimes I still believed we would marry each other. But mostly I remembered the way it was.

"How are you?" he asks.

"Okay. I dreamed you were sleeping with my sister again."

"Which one?"

"Hannah."

"Huh."

"It's either a dream of jealousy or betrayal." I could sense him withdraw from the word *betrayal*.

The day he helped me move he smoked three joints in two hours, and I told him I was smarter than he was.

Then I said, "You betrayed me."

"*I* betrayed *you?*"

"You broke my heart." I looked right at him to see if he'd flinch.

"I'm sorry, Emily." He didn't.

He always smashed the fantasy. Why couldn't he just say, *You broke mine too*, which was true. No one gets out undamaged.

We were silent and his body seemed to shake. I wondered if he felt powerful for being the one to actually leave. But then, how many times does someone have to say, *I can't love you the way you are*, before it gets to be really obvious you've gotta go? I could have just as easily said, *How can you love me the way I am?* It's unbearable how simple we are.

Truth being the ability to know or intuit before the mind explains in words, in sentences, in story.

I watch a bird fly and realize I'm grown up. I sit in myself like a ship waiting to set sail. Keats wrote a poem about an urn on which two lovers were painted, caught for eternity a moment away from a kiss. It was intense for him to think about that urn and those lovers, detained in that moment of anticipation. To him it was the best place to be—in expectancy—not during, not after, but filled with the lust and desire of possibility. Love was fantasy, a way to escape, and when it lost this charm . . . what was left?

I watch a bird fly and never know from where to where. I know its fluttering surprise and instant loss. I am grown up now with nowhere to hide but in my ship without sails. I decide today not to blame anyone, not even myself. I will accept it, all of it, the entire world as she rests, with no beginning, no end. Eliot wrote, "In my beginning is my end," and when I read *Four Quartets*, the bowl of fuchsia peonies on the coffee table is enough to make me cry. I had not known such flowers existed. He writes:

> What might have been is an abstraction
> Remaining a perpetual possibility
> Only in a world of speculation.
> What might have been and what has been
> Point to one end, which is always present.

⚘ ⚘ ⚘ ⚘

I couldn't stop. I didn't try for a long time. I remember my room on the third floor of my Greene Street apartment, where I lived when I first moved to Vermont. I drank bottles and bottles of stunning red wine. Every day, an afterthought. I kept a rigorous schedule back then: philosophy, poetry, fiction, astrology. One hour each per day. Coffee and cigarettes every morning like a saving grace. No matter how awful I felt in the morning, no matter how bad it had been the night before, by evening I convinced myself to do it again.

Our room was robin's-egg blue, the room where I lost myself. I had been losing it for a decade. Seven years had passed since the lonely basement room of winter, but sometimes the pain of addiction turns to desperation. In that desperation, we surrender. There were so many colors in our room: rainbow rug I called biblical, blue china cabinet, red chairs, green table, and rust-red blanket. White paraded around the edges of everything. I remember now how nothing was left sacred; nothing was too far.

I'd get going around six or seven every night. In the end, I mostly drank alone. By the time Josh got there I'd be bleeding all over the floors and the bed. With the kitchen knives, I sliced my arms (really, they were only scratches) wanting my insides to fall out. It was this act, looking back, that was a sign of me still there, still trying to make my disease known by wanting its scars visible on the canvas of my skin. I loathed the world for the so-called

boundaries imposed on my body and the secrecy of my inner pain
trapped there in the pith and marrow of it all, unseen.

My eyes glazed. I could tell by Josh's face when he came in that
I was a ghost to him. But Josh always said, *It's still you, Emily. It's
a disease, but it's* your *disease.* Though I'm sure he found a softer
way of saying it because he never wanted to hurt anyone.

I remember the day: I worked at the homeless shelter for the
mentally ill, where there was nothing to do but watch TV or go
online because the clients mostly stayed in their rooms. I got home
at five and started drinking a bottle of vodka I'd stashed under the
kitchen sink. Around eight I brushed my teeth and walked to the
liquor store for a jug of wine. The smoke from my cigarette bil-
lowed in the chilly February air. I felt perfectly alone. I remember thinking that I could be happy forever if I just never ran out of
booze and cigarettes. A fleeting thought, but a regular one.

Nothing about this night was different from any other night.
Josh returned home from work around ten and wanted to go to
bed. I got upset because I didn't want the night to end—I never
did. Couldn't he stay up and have a drink with me, couldn't he at
least talk to me? Our apartment was only one room, so it was hard
for him to avoid me.

I punched Josh in the face that night. His eyes blinked like a
flashing red light. Later, years later, he told me it didn't hurt. But
what did that matter? He pushed me out of his way and ran out.
I tried to follow him barefoot through the snow. He screamed
and retreated—wounded, tamed for the moment. It felt like hours
passed before he returned, lying down on the biblical rug, the coat
of many colors, and cried me out of him. That was the end. It came
as no relief to me. For a week, he stayed; every night he turned his
back to me in bed and every night I lay with my hand on his back
feeling the warmth of his body. How could this body leave me?

He cleaned the room, bought groceries, wrote me a note, and
left. Beside the note he neatly folded a green scarf that he'd bought
me for Christmas, months ago.

I started getting sober in the blue room, just before he left. I told Josh, I promised him, but he said it didn't matter. He needed to be alone. Quitting is hard and not using gets easier but learning to live feels intolerable because of all the emotions I'd stuffed for the past fifteen years. A woman named Sarah, who became my friend, came to pick me up and drive me to recovery meetings.

"Just don't drink," she'd say when she dropped me off, "and say a prayer tonight."

"Okay," I'd say and sigh, my hand on the door handle. I didn't want to leave the warmth of her car, though it smelled of sour milk and dog. "Okay, thanks."

"You take care now."

The hell of it goes on. You have to figure out how to survive without escaping as you had always escaped. The people I met told me it would get better and that I should go to a meeting every day and say a prayer every night. I did whatever they told me to do.

Josh had this idea that getting high enhanced life and only through drugs could he reach true artistic brilliance. Thinking about it now, I want to laugh. I used to say, "Listen to yourself, listen to your mind, just sit and listen for a minute. There's no brilliance there."

I learned that brilliance is not of the mind but of another place, the soft place that you cultivate in your own silence. The place you get to when you understand that words only point at the truth, language will never do, but it is all we have. Brilliance is the dark night where you face yourself alone, sober, silent.

How it felt to get sober: A body is forced through the surface, a body that has lived submerged in water for years. It doesn't know how to breathe in air. The sun in its open eyes burns. The body tries to dive back down over and over, to escape again. But once you know, once you leave the blue room, you resurface. You can't go back without tying a brick to your foot. People do it all the time or, in truth, most of the time; they tie on the brick and fill their pockets with stones, sinking away. But the body can't return to the ease of underwater living; the body knows now it is drowning.

I see the disease of addiction in people's eyes—my own in theirs—sense it on their skin, smell it. I feel the blade of it in their embrace, the force of it. To see it now, in another person, terrifies me. I know the emptiness, the complete and utter desperation, and the denial. I know the feeling of helplessness that makes walking past the liquor store without going in to stand in the aisles filled with bottles—glistening, beautiful, lethal—impossible. I know that an addict will push anyone away who might make her recognize herself. I believed that was the reason Josh left. Only when he realized I was going to meetings did he refuse to stay. Even though it was what he said he wanted for me, he couldn't watch it. He knew what it meant for him.

Truth being the ability to hold two seemingly oppositional ideas at once and know they are both true.

I search the apartment for Josh paraphernalia to burn. Pictures, notes, cards—even the one in which he wrote, "I will cook you eggs until I die," I want to burn. Then I remember another lover, from long ago. T and I were lying in bed together and he said that we should get to know each other better.

"Okay," I said, annoyed. We'd known each other for years.

"How do you like your eggs?"

"I don't eat eggs," I lied.

When I left T, who also had a live-in girlfriend, I left the country. A part of me was searching for my father the way women sometimes do. Either she marries him or finds him within herself. She learns to accept him or her love for him as she does for herself. Twenty years old, it was Italy, with all her beautiful women and charmed men, her color and gold, with her sullen waterways and stark piazzas and Mary Our Holy Mother of the Sea. In Venice, I rendered my profile in oil pastels and walked the tiny village with the other tourists, watching them scatter pigeons for pictures or sit in the café where Hemingway wrote or Pound drank or Ginsberg quoted a Greek play.

My father's voice hummed in my ear, his fisher king heart sitting near me whispered how I should have come with a friend. He said, *Oh Emily, how could you run off like this?* At night, I passed the jolly-hearted hollers of intoxicated men. I sat at a tiny square table alone and finished a bottle of wine. I watched the sky crumble away, the moon leak out, and heard my father say, *Oh Emily, don't take any of these men to bed, they'll be gone in the morning—you aren't going to fall in love in Venice, you fool!* "Leave me alone," I whispered, "let me be as I am."

I never found my father there and it would be years before I realized his voice was really my own. Later, I chose to love Josh because I thought he would never leave me, never hurt me, let me be as I am—a drunk . . . mean . . . cruel even? I thought he was nothing like my father. Wasn't it Josh who taught me that to love meant to enter the unknown, vulnerable without armor? It was not desire—the lust for movement and thus escape—but the steady acceptance of vulnerability and the willingness to forgive. But was it Josh who taught me this or did I learn it alone, in my new apartment where I painted the walls gold and listened to the barking dogs, the scent of grilled meat drifting in through the window?

Eliot wrote:

> Go, go, go, said the bird: human kind
> Cannot bear very much reality
> Time past and time future
> What might have been and what has been
> Point to one end, which is always present.

Know that they are both true at once—neither negates the other.

When fall arrives I am four months sober. I watch the birds fumble in the sky. This new person, the sober me, roots. By spring, I say, will I bud? I go to recovery meetings, I pray. I try to forget Josh. I see him on the street with other women. He lets their hands drop from his when he sees me, he moves away from them, to me—don't they notice—touches my shoulder, hugs me. I resent him, the resentment feels toxic. I know he still loves me. He knows I love him.

Today he runs across the street from the café where we first met. There are tears in his eyes. What is it? I tell him to be true to himself. He looks at me for a long time. I notice how thin he's become. I don't know the color of his eyes—blue, green, hazel—if we had children would they have his long lashes? I hold him against my chest, his body a drug to me. I don't know how my body will ever release his: his smell, a nutmeggy pine, the touch of skin and his roughened hands, all like gorgeous bottles of red wine.

The morning after I punched Josh and he cried me out of him on the biblical rug of a million colors, I called my father. Blood from my period smeared the floor in the robin's-egg blue room. I wore Josh's T-shirt, the one my sister and her husband gave him for Christmas.

My father said, "Emily, Josh loves you."

"No, no, I hurt him, Dad. I hurt him so much . . . I can't stop drinking."

Silence, and then he says, "You've got to stop. You can't live like this. Who wants to live like that?"

No one. No one.

I walked up the hill to the old blue room, whispering prayers to the wind. It was spring then but the leaves had not begun to bud. Sometimes I repeated, *by the grace of God*, as I walked. In my room, I lay in the tumbled mess of bedsheets, traced my fingers over the wine stains from when I threw a glass in Josh's face. "God," I whisper, "please." The grief is unbearable.

I read Bill Holm's *Playing the Black Piano*, a book of poems my mother sent me. He writes about the sea in his poem "The Sea Eats What It Pleases."

> But the sea does not hate you, or imagine
> That you have wounded it with your avarice.

. . . .

Only humans, so newly risen from fish,
Imagine drowning each other for reasons.

It is not the rhythm of Holm that speaks to me, though it keeps me and holds me to it, but the idea that cannot be explained, only sensed in this question: Why do we imagine that the pain we inflict on each other has meaning?

I move through entire days where it is enough just to stay sober. At the end of winter, I go down to the lake and spend hours photographing rolling waves of ice. Below them the lake thaws, yet the surface is still hinged with enormous plates of ice that won't let the underwater out. With force, the water churns beneath the ice, moves the ice-crested surface in waves that roll and hurl against the cement walls of the shore, breaking down little by little.

That Kind of Blue

She stands on the deck of the cabin at Burnt Shanty Lake, a half-silhouette in the waning light of August. We are in our twenties. Grandma's still alive, our sisters with us, her mother healthy. The cabin is still the place to which we all return, a longed-for destination full of childhood memories and girlhood. I see her there surrounded by all of us—sisters, mothers, Grandma: our world of matriarchy.

Only once have I returned to the lake cabin our grandfather built in the 1950s since she hid there with the skinny man she still loves, stealing wood from the neighbors for a November fire that would have done little for those uninsulated rooms. Getting messed up the way we once did together, but too far gone now. Alone, in different eras, other members of our family have done the same—the disease running thick in our blood and the cabin deep in the woods.

Soon the cabin will be gone, sold to a rich doctor from out east. They will most likely bulldoze it and erect a quaint but modern replacement. The sidewalk where we pressed our hands in wet cement and wrote our names—me, the oldest, first; she, second in our line of cousins, following close behind—broken up, hauled away. Would the new children find our path through the birch trees to the point of land jutting out at the end of the bay, so easily seen by our mothers from the deck of the cabin or the dock, the place we called "the point" that had been our own mothers' fort as girls? Would they run barefoot, leaping over the tree roots that snaked from the earth, all the way there? And would they take care to avoid the swampy water near the path's edge where she and I once swam and stepping out of the lake discovered our legs were covered in thick black leeches? We lay in the grass fake screaming while our mothers shook salt on the offending creatures.

⁂⁂⁂⁂

From my desk, I look out the window at the winter trees reflected in the broken ice of puddles—they look fogged and half-imaginary. In looking I find longing, a body of pain. I long for the trigger that shuts down the thinking mind, lets us live there in the currents of the underworld, lower brain, place of ancestry and myth. A place we drank to get to. But in sobriety, I have discovered certain clouds on windy days in blue-fielded skies transport me there. Certain memories, if only for a moment—pockets of blue, I call them.

You, I want to tell her, *would know this sky if I told you that its color—blue like the veins of our skin—tastes of water and sun, and those clouds smell like the lake when we were children and dove down into it searching for pretty stones, holding our breath as long as we could, playing underwater tea party. We swam until our eyes stung and heads burned from the sun and we were so tired that all we wanted was to sit in our mothers' laps—their warm legs slick with tanning oil— curled against their breasts for one eternal moment. You would understand that kind of blue.*

There in the blue of sky—a limbo of sensory memory and other-worldliness—time folds in on itself, shuts down, and we float free—soul and body free. I meet her there, in the other world, the world before, one of childhood water and sun, footpath to fort, sauna and mother love.

⁂⁂⁂⁂

"My son needs me. I'm going to quit," she says into the phone, half a country between us. It's been months since anyone has heard from her.

"I thought I would never see you again," I tell her. Sitting on the floor of my kitchen, my body taut and anxious. I can hear my husband speaking softly in the next room.

"I know, me too. Sorry, man."

I am desperate to say the right thing. But the distance between us evades connection. The fear of losing her, too much. Her own survival takes precedence over tending to the pain of those who love her.

I stare at the red wall of my kitchen and think about Burnt Shanty Lake and our childhood together. I try to remember a day before her mom got sick and Grandma died, before I nearly drank myself to death and she almost died in a hospital bed with a hole in her arm, before her son refused to speak to her, before the truth of the world made itself clear—nothing stays.

For a long time, I thought I could save her. But ours is not that kind of disease, the saving kind. It's a disease so dense with long-ing, so wanton with desire, that even in the end stages of addiction and alcoholism, the addict still believes she can return to that first high—that first heaven. Even years since I quit, I feel that familiar pattern of want creep into my days like a pulse flickering alive, its all-consuming desire for more.

In the pink cloud of our youth we drank cheap champagne, un-aware of its lethal effects on our bodies, bleached our hair, and lay in flimsy swimwear greased with tanning oil until our limbs turned golden, our cheeks rosy. We spent all evening dressing up to go out but never ended up leaving. Or, leaving, we drove in someone's shit car over dirt roads, passing a bottle of something cheap and harsh, smoking cigarettes, sharing lip gloss. The soft purr of the gravel road whispered through the open car windows.

We crooned off-key to Hank Williams Jr.'s "Family Tradition" (our anthem), Kid Rock, Janis Joplin, OutKast, the Indigo Girls. We'd find a street dance in one of the small midwestern mining towns that lay like constellations around open-pit iron ore mines in northern Minnesota. Golden bodied, drunk, faces painted, we careened through crowds with our shoulders grazing, arms looped as though we were one body, one wild creature set free.

꒰ ꒱ ꒰ ꒱

Days later, she's gone. Slipped back into the fold. I imagine her in an oversized red parka that might keep her from freezing in the winter night. I see her walking beside him along the edge of Lake Superior in the city of Duluth. The lake beyond them is so vast it goes on forever.

I sit at my desk transfixed until the vision of her half-silhouette resurfaces in my mind. I see her turning, the fog rising off of the lake at dawn—had we been up all night? We were young and earlier that night Grandma danced with my sister Hannah, a slow spin around the unfinished living room of the Burnt Shanty Lake cabin. The walls still wore the *Life* magazine covers Grandpa had posted between beams—Ronald Reagan, Jimmy Carter, JFK—as they always would. We were all there: her son, our moms and sisters, maybe even my little brother, listening to John Prine sing about the big, old, happy world, and we were happy. Happy enough.

The sky of morning was so blue with you there in it. I don't know where you are and I won't for weeks or months even. Blue, I think, like the ancestry of this disease in our blood, blue like our matching eyes, blue like the lake water of our youth, blue like memory, that kind of blue.

I don't want to feel the familiar panic that you might be dead. I am calling your name, calling you back. We are running through the darkened woods, at the cabin playing flashlight tag with the neighbor girls and our sisters. Running toward the road through the tall grass where your mom once took us to play "lions and tigers and bears, oh my!" The fireflies are flickering and somewhere close a campfire burns. I am calling your name, calling you back. You could turn and you could look and you could stop. And you can't.

The Birds

The birds are committing suicide at the window again. Today I found a northern flicker on the porch below the bay window that looks out over the lake. Still alive, fluttering. I bent to scoop the bird and realized I have not been a child for a long time. But here in my childhood home in northern Minnesota, where we—the newly wed—have come to spend part of the summer, I feel the distance shrink between me and that other world. Josh watches me through the big window. But he turns away when I notice him. We have just arrived from our honeymoon, a road trip down the Pacific Coast that began in Oregon and ended near San Francisco. Will memory befriend me here? I wonder, as I watch the dying bird. Days later, I am still uncertain.

My four sisters, brother, and I grew up in this house beside a lake. We lived five years in its small walkout basement while Dad cut and stacked the logs above. The intermittent whine of the chainsaw reminded us that he was there, and when he came down for dinner he smelled like sawdust and a mixture of gas and oil. Sometimes a thin layer of sawdust stuck in the stubble of his cheeks. His hands, even after he scrubbed them, remained oil stained. For years, I associated that particular smell with my father. He was an ambitious builder and loved the act of creation, which was not how he made money, but how he built a life for himself and his family. It was from him I learned to love the satisfaction of creation, and hard work.

Yet the older I got the more I struggled to navigate my relationship with my father. I was fifteen the year we moved into our finished home, the year after my brother was born; by then I was already trying to escape the world he and my mother had created for us. Rebellion, perhaps. In me lived an instinct for freedom, a longing for another world, stronger than the partial comforts of his.

🐦 🐦 🐦 🐦

After years of small apartments and basement living, we felt like monarchs when we finally moved in upstairs. My sister Hannah and I shared a bedroom on the first floor—we slept in twin beds that had belonged to my father's grandmother—perhaps a century old. We lay awake at night talking in the dark until one of us fell asleep. Some nights those conversations felt like love medicine—part healing balm, part flickering fire of sisterhood. Even today when I sleep in that old bedroom my dreams become more vivid as though imbued with the intensity of my adolescent mind, a mind that seamlessly moved between imagination and the grown-up world of fact and fiction. A mind that sought to understand the limits of her freedom and surpass them.

As girls, in the woods beyond the house, we found forests of soft moss and tall mangy pines, fields of marshland where we lay watching the sky. Our golden retriever bounded ahead of us, sniffing deer tracks, circling the forest for prey. We told the tales children tell—imagined worlds made to understand the real one—hiding away our souls from the dull eyes of grown-ups, who so easily smudged us out with their demands for order and assimilation. Stories laced these hours, carrying me through childhood. And once, I told myself not to forget what it was like to be a child because clearly all the grown-ups had, but I have since found only nostalgia for this place, long gone the girl governed by the forest and the laws of nature.

To the west lies the lake; to the east, the pond. North, the marshlands of the bog oppose our neighbors at the southern border. But all around the house the marsh creeps in, a thick bog with pine growing up through the moss. A former neighbor told my father that a young girl drowned in the pond. As a child, I often found my way down to the old whiskey still near the pond. It was here the girl named Anna was said to have been going on her last day. A small indent in the hill remains the only evidence of the still—was it real? I found some scrap metal and an antique clothes ringer for drying. I tried to imagine Anna, what she might have looked like, how she dressed. But sometimes I thought it was just a story my father made up to keep us away from the pond. I never once swam in those murky waters for fear of Anna's boney arm grabbing my small ankle, pulling me down forever into the bottomless muck of her grave. She must be very lonely, I thought, lonely and sad.

At night in the boathouse room beside the lake, Josh and I hear the yelp of wolves passing through. I pull him closer to me in bed. I am not scared but mystified by what is still wild and untamed. I look for the bodies of harvested deer when I walk in the woods. I wonder where the wolves have gone.

Mostly, though, I listen for the howl of loons at night, a wail that sounds similar to the howl of the wolf, or the yodel of male loons in mating season that vibrates in the dark acoustics of the still lake. There's no other sound of night more intimate or more haunting to me than the call of the loon. All my life I have known that cry that punctuates the twin edges of night—it calls and propels me toward summer and the lakes of my youth.

As girls, we could sometimes go swimming alone. "How deep?" I asked my father once when we were driving to another cabin, where he planned to play a game of basketball while we swam. "Up to your chest," my father said. I pressed him for specificity, wondering if chest meant neck or navel—what was the region—it seemed important to my eight-year-old mind. "To your nipples," he said, and then he and his brother broke into laughter. The kind of laughter that shrinks a girl of any age, renders her helpless.

I looked down at my short, thin legs. It was not the first joke made about the female body that I had absorbed, partly shocked, partly shamed. My mother's body seemed to be under constant scrutiny: the size of her breasts, her arms, her belly, the shape of her, the thinness. Mostly, the words were couched in humor, which did not soften the blow, but at times the words seemed of a harsher current, the scrutiny more blatant. At five feet five inches tall, she weighed ninety-eight pounds the day she married my father. A doctor once told her she could never have children, but she had six and five of us are women. Still, in a house full of women, the undercurrent remained, threading us to a self-hatred that we would never fully outswim.

Back in the car, did my sisters laugh about nipples? Alida wasn't paying attention, but Hannah looked at me, waiting for my reaction. I looked down, filled with shame, hoping never again to encounter my father's eyes in the rearview mirror.

I loved to swim as a child. Dad and I often traversed the lake, our arms flopping, legs kicking. Swimming. Dark nights with the starry field above the lake, reflecting down, calling me away from this world. My father jumping from the moving pontoon boat, jumping from the end of the dock, underwater for miles and miles it seemed. I never understood his sense of humor, the undertone of something I found humiliating at times.

I would later sense this same feeling in a writing workshop when a male teacher asked a female writer, "Where's this character's penis?" By which he meant, his sex drive, as though a story about a man required a constant tracking of his desire to fuck and no woman could understand that. Or when another male teacher wondered who would want to read a story that was only about women's lives. *All women. Everywhere.*

They were nice men, these teachers; likewise, my father is a very kind and loving man. Yet it was his way of seeing women in the world that hurt me. I adored my father and yet. In the dark of the woods, I hid from him. I looked without knowing, for a place of escape, for relief.

Swimming. I learned to swim early enough to not remember a time when I didn't. Back and forth, back and forth, wherever I was: a lake, somewhere, any lake, everywhere, but not the pond, never the pond. Swimming, like the loons I so loved, I was a different creature in water; it was a different world.

➤➤❧❧

Out on the lake, a fishing boat trolls. Josh sleeps in the boathouse by the shore. Today it will rain, even storm. I wonder how our love will evolve. How will he treat our daughters; will he unlearn the ways he's been taught to hurt women, ways he might not yet recognize?

I watch a sparrow in the yard from my window and realize I am lucky with birds. I watch the sparrow in the yard as I hang the swim towels and realize the world is lucky with birds. Nights in the boathouse are filled with dreams of betrayal. I notice only certain "ones" betray. But these include my husband. In the morning I turn and lay my hand on his shoulder, you're still here? You're still here. I realize betrayal takes many forms. I have never easily forgiven those who betray me, though, perhaps, eventually we all betray in one way or another.

Today a purple finch thumps the window. I go out. I hold the finch in my palms. She looks like a sparrow to me, tumbled from the sky. I lay her on the wooden picnic table and blood comes from inside to trickle out her beak. She struggles to fly in the face of death. She shudders one of her feathers loose—a small offering to the ground.

Her official name, purple finch, comes from her Latin title, *Carpodacus purpureus*. Not purple, *purpureus*, a crimson, which means nothing to her, female, because only the male *Carpodacus purpureus* sports red plumage. I walk through the yard, a sand lot, to the shallow water of the lake. At the shore the boathouse stands quietly, awaiting my return to sleep.

All around me the dark forest and the bog, which could be as deep as the pond beneath its moss layers, creeps close. I want to bury the finch, to light a tiny fire in her honor, but I toss her into the woods instead. I toss her far into the bog where she will be eaten; better the dead are given back to the living. From the lakeshore, I look up at the house with all its window-eyes shifting shadows. I can see a bird's-eye view, a certain window looking like a door into another world, a patch of sky kingdom. Who wouldn't risk her life for her own kingdom of sky? Who wouldn't at least try? The window, then, a murderer, reflecting back to us that sky. All of it a matter of perception—a way of seeing that marked whether or not we would thrive or merely survive.

I return to the kitchen table, where I sit alone and think about trees. The birch in the yard grows eyes the size of a baby's fist, its bark a stunning white against the storm-laden sky. White pines have the softest needles. My father is lucky with trees; he has planted thousands and thousands of pines in his life. He tried to teach me to identify them when I was a girl and it felt like a game to me. But I imagine if I had gotten one wrong I would have insisted that I didn't want to play anymore, insisted that I didn't care because what better defense is there than fuck it, which became my banner for so many years.

Outside the kitchen window over the sink, a row of Norway pines separates the yard from the forest beyond. No one goes out there anymore. My mother says I helped her plant them in the rain, but though I want to, I do not remember.

🐦🐦🐦🐦

As a child, I became a detective of sorts. What my father would call a "sneak," and it was true I was a child thief at times. I believed there were certain things I should have and if I didn't have them, I would simply take them. Once, he caught me stealing peanut M&M'S from his coworker after he stepped away from behind the pharmacy counter. "Why would you do that?" he asked. This would become a common question between us in later years, perhaps even still. At the time, I felt ashamed but also dumbfounded: I wanted them, that is why.

What was I looking for back then?

So much.

What was unseen to me that I could sense all around me, always present.

I wanted to know.

What was wrong with me? Why did I feel things more intensely than others deemed appropriate?

In one of my first memories I am two or three years old and I color all over the back of my bedroom door in red and blue crayons. When I proudly show my father my work of art he punishes me. It seems like a stunning betrayal. But I don't know if this memory is true or not; what I felt then cannot be what I feel now. If I close my eyes I can still see the door, still see the swirls of red and blue. Still feel the shock of his displeasure. So, what truth matters? Whose? And is this act of confession a deeper betrayal? Why do I hold these memories inside of me, always like stones dropped into a deep pond? Stones so smooth and round and glistening from all these years grinding them down.

What they kept from me made me weary as a child. There was something about most grown-ups that I didn't trust—they were liars and teased me. Thus, I kept a part of me hidden away. Waiting for the secret to reveal itself, for the true tale to unwind, I started to divide. What was really me remained folded inward, a secret, different from the me I presented or let be observed.

I pressed my ear to the door of my bedroom, listening long minutes to the conversations my mother had with her sister, her sister-in-law, my father when she thought I had long been asleep. Someone was getting divorced; my father forgot the wine; the sorrow of my mother as she watched her father slip away to cancer in a few short months. The sound of her sobs muffled, almost silent. What she kept from me, I still carried—a dark mass, a shadow body, a cloak.

I ran away into the dark woods. There was nothing in the woods that scared me. Rather, the silence, along with the occasional snap of branches from squirrels and the echo of a thrush's song, comforted me. Filled with anger and self-pity, I'd lie in the moss beds of the bog and watch the moon shift amid the clouds until I grew cold enough or lonely enough to return home.

⁂⁂⁂⁂

My father is in the kitchen fixing a sandwich when my brother tells me about his basketball huddle. My brother sits over a plate of hot dogs on buns with ketchup. He's wearing a baggy T-shirt, let's say, and long jersey shorts. His toes probably grip the rung of the stool and he grunts as he tells the story.

"When we get down in the huddle, after they call out the starters, you know, right before tip-off, the team captain starts saying, 'We're going to kill them, we're going to rape their women, we're going to eat their babies.'" He pauses to bite into another hot dog. "It's from a movie," he says and continues eating.

Dad grunts from across the kitchen.

I sigh and say, "Really, that is ridiculous, Aden." There are other words I'd use to describe this but I'm tentative, skeptical, and I don't quite understand.

"That's just how guys are," Dad chimes in.

I sigh and say, "Absolutely not!"

No, I'm silent.

My father grunts. My brother shrugs. What can he do?

This is an outrage. No, it's just the way guys are. An outrage. No just the way . . . Outrage.

My father doesn't understand why this passive acceptance of violence abuses me, just like he doesn't understand why joking that female weather reporters should announce the weather in bikinis hurts women—his daughters and wife, specifically. Like me, my father is sensitive to criticism; he sulks, remains withdrawn and sullen in the aftermath of my critiques. In part, it is this critique of him—my anger over his sexism—that has made it difficult for us to form a close relationship. Both perceive betrayal in the other.

When my brother was a child, my father taught him that "girls are sissies and boys are tough," or some version of this ridiculous myth of patriarchy. Home from my first year of college, I over-heard him offering up this lesson to his five-year-old son. It seemed like something out of a cartoon, something so stupid it didn't warrant a response. But I wanted to protect my little brother. I didn't want him to share my father's fate, his fear and misunderstanding of women.

"Dad, really, why are you telling him that?" I asked.

"Heh," he laughed at me. "It's just easier, Emily. You want your little brother to go to school and get picked on?"

What about doing the right thing? I should have said. Isn't that what you taught me? Didn't you say that I can do whatever boys can do? Didn't you buy me a racetrack for my sixth birthday, which I took back to the store and exchanged for a sled only after crying myself to sleep because in my child brain I thought that I was betraying you. Even then I knew the boundaries of gender and the ways we tried to both subvert and protect them as though our lives depended on knowing.

In truth, Aden never told me the story of the basketball huddle. We never sat together like that in the kitchen, though I imagine it would have gone that way. It was a sister who relayed the private story. A secret, like so many other things kept secret in our house: the silent pain of girls not eating, or eating too much—the body turning inward, away, attached to the myth of its survival, making it impossible for a woman to thrive.

The stark contrast of the said against the unsaid in any home casts a deepening shadow. But the poison rot of the secrets women are made to carry pin us to the ground before we ever have a chance. It is in this way, we lose ourselves, our potential and capacity blighted out, clipped. So often remembering feels like the wind knocked out of me. Like I have fallen from the sky.

How to reconcile the transgressions of the beloved? I'll never know. Nor how to weigh the sins of my own betrayal of those I love against my survival. I want so much to be loved unconditionally—I want to love this way—but I am telling you this so that you know, because you must know, that the truth of your experience is necessarily your own and no one else's.

҈ ҈ ҈ ҈

Last night the wind whorled through the windows of our boathouse cabin. Josh sat reading on the sofa and I in the bed. In the morning, the light would be clean, the air like fresh bedsheets around the ankle and chin, the smell of late summer moving in across the lake, the water cooler. Last night, we woke to the storm: rain pounding earth. I went out under the eaves of the boathouse to watch the rain on the water, on the beach sand. It would soak through me in an instant had I stood in it.

Last night I went out to piss in the yard. The moon was high above the scrappy pines, laying a shadow over everything, a magic powder, a dust of light. I kept thinking, *Where can you find this? Where can you find this?* And I knew those were the words of my father; the part of him that I adored was also the part of him that loved these woods and that made a world in which he hoped I'd thrive.

Out along the lakeshore where the blueberries grow in August, I walked and walked as a girl. This house, this place was nothing like where we'd lived before: the moss-bedded forest, the bog, the pond, the shore of white sand and pines constituted a secret outer world, a place of freedom. I wandered every inch of this new land, returning again and again to the pond, where I would stand looking, squinting to imagine the lost girl, Anna: the girl at the bottom of the pond.

In the winter, when the pond froze, we skated on the ice and cross-country skied around its outer edge. Alone in the morning, one winter, drawn to the secluded world of the woods surrounding my house, I took my skates down to the pond after an early freeze. It hadn't yet snowed so I could skate around the entire pond on clear ice. I trudged through the frozen bog, trying to step lightly and not sink through. It wasn't dangerous, but I didn't like the feeling of losing ground. I sat down to lace my skates on a log beside the pond, the morning sun glistened off the clumps of snow hanging from the pines that stood like frozen guards of winter: my secret world. I skated out on the pond, the ice almost perfect; it would be another decade before I found pond ice this good, another lifetime.

I wasn't much good as a skater, though I'd taken lessons. I was a better swimmer. But alone I could make-believe I skated marvelously, and who would know otherwise? I skated backward, grooving figure eights, circling, twirling, and pretending to land jumps and bowing to an imagined crowd. But when I tripped, the hard reality of the ice floor gripped me. I lay there on my back breathing hard, watching the white puffs of air float out of me: my knees aching, wrists wincing. My cheeks and toes so cold I wanted to cry.

When I turned to get up, there in the ice I saw a fish frozen as though caught in motion. Its tail curled, its eyes wide open. I rubbed the ice with my mitten for a minute thinking I could free it. The fish's back was speckled, the ice along the underside of its body was cracked and crystals had formed an opaque, shimmering edge around its body, which seemed to leap.

It would snow that night and I would never find the fish again. I blew hot air into the ice above it, rubbed with my mitten, pressed my nose against the ice, and pounded my fists. It was beautiful—that fish trapped in flight—I wanted it for my own as much as I wanted to free it. I did not yet understand the nature of beauty, the cost.

🐦 🐦 🐦 🐦

I am leaving today. Josh left a week earlier to return to work. Last night the moon came out to greet me. I stood in the yard and

watched the light reflected on the lake. I listened for the lone call
of a loon, knowing it was too late in the season to hear them but
wanting one last cry—one last echo into the myths of time, the
ache and sweep of all that passes and passes through.

Years ago, after I'd moved away to Vermont from Minnesota,
I felt so close to this edge. Drinking nightly, fantasizing about my
own death, cutting myself, isolated and alone, I would call my father. Sometimes I would call him at work during the day and he
would say, "Hang on a sec, Em." I could hear him walking across
the squeaky pharmacy floor, through the back rooms, down into
the basement with the cordless phone. I could picture that basement strewn with boxes and furniture, belongings from generations of our family. They left the stuff they no longer wanted but
could not get rid of, as though knowing that one's old dolls still existed somewhere safeguarded us from loss.

Dad never said he couldn't talk, he never said he was too
busy, and he always told me it would be okay. It would get better. Though, I am not sure he believed that himself. Once he said,
"You're enough just the way you are." I can't piece together the
other parts of that conversation, but I was sitting on my cousin's
living room floor in Vermont looking at my suitcase when he told
me that. It startled me at the time. I wanted to believe him, but
all the evidence I'd collected over the years weaved another story.
Still, his dedication comforted me. I always knew I was loved.

In the woods, barefoot, I search the ground for the finch, the
moon lighting my way. Though I know she's long been devoured,
I still need to look for her. I still long to find her body, to give her
a proper burial—light a pyre in her honor, let this old way burn
out. I think of the body of my own mother, a living body, my first
home and the life that first nurtured my own. And then I think of
the Greek myth of the birds: In the time before the world came to
be, there was only air, sky, and flying birds. Many kinds of birds.
I imagine air as sea, sky as water, a swimming of flight. The lark's
father dies, but there is no ground in which to bury him, no place

to store his sacred remains. The birds gather together in the sky-sea, trying to think of what to do. But they can think of nothing. So, the lark, knowing she must do something to save her father's honor, decides she will bury the body of her father in the back of her mind, and this, they say, is the beginning of memory.

Prayer for the Woman
Murdered in My Neighborhood

Kathleen was murdered in her home. The police aren't saying how, or what happened. In the afternoon meeting today, held in the church basement—the one with the wall of Jesus Christs of various ethnicities—a man whispered, "She had a really nice house." One woman raised her hand, "I'm afraid. I have two little kids. I don't know what to do." Then other women raised their hands; they too did not know what to do. The man who was running the meeting, a famous trumpet player, said he'd noticed women in his neighborhood looking fearfully at him. He didn't blame them; it had been a week since her murder. He had wanted to talk about solitude in the meeting, but we never did. He had said: let's talk about when loneliness turns into solitude.

Outside Kathleen's home the neighbors build a shrine, and sometimes, just before dark, the shrine becomes a vigil: mourners holding candles on the sidewalk. Today I stopped at the light on the corner and looked over at the shrine, but I did not go to it. A partial shelter has been erected: a canvas ceiling over candles, cards, flowers, prayer flags. Yesterday I stopped to see the shrine and sat to light a candle. A friend leaves a fresh cup of homemade cappuccino each morning. I wanted to leave a note but could think of nothing to write, and when I noticed the police coming from her bright yellow house I hurried away. She was a fifty-year-old woman living alone but for her dog.

A few years ago, I met Kathleen at the social services organization where she had been employed for quite some time. I was a substitute in the house where she worked. It was a house for people with disabilities.

Kathleen told me a story about her life in Boston, her time being a sub like me. She was specific, exact, dedicated. "I used to call in each afternoon and tell them I was free that night," she said. "They still had to go down their list, but I think they went a lot faster knowing I was available. That's how I got the subbing jobs in Boston and eventually got hired." I listened to her and wondered how someone could be so committed to work at a low-paying, dull, mostly thankless social work job. I didn't admire her; rather, I was fearful that I would become her. We were sitting in the tiny office of the house and it smelled like someone's rotten lunch. She explained how to dispense meds and showed me the book I needed to write everything down in. Residents came in periodically to get meds or ask a question or shoot the shit. Kathleen liked the residents. She treated them well and her body moved easily around them. As we walked through the house, Kathleen called out their names like they were her roommates, and yet she kept her distance. "It's bad social work to befriend clients," she said and shook her head. I could not tell if she believed this declaration or not. But Kathleen was pretty much the ideal worker for her position. I admired her that.

Kathleen lived in a small house on Park Street in the Old North End. She had painted the outside lively colors: turquoise, yellow, and purple. She kept a garden in her tiny backyard. I stood in the garden with a friend, days after she'd passed. There were two metal chairs for sitting. "She's still here," my friend said and touched the Tibetan prayer flags hanging between the fence and the garage. Those flags that everyone in the town hung from their porches and windows were thought to send prayers with each flap in the wind. Thousands of prayers flew up on a windy day. Their five colors are arranged in order: blue, white, red, green, and yellow. Each color represents a different element—sky and space, air and wind, fire, water, earth. In Tibet, balance of the elements will create good health and a life of harmony.

I thought of Kathleen then, how she rode her bike to work and always wore a helmet. How her son was grown and visited often. My friend and I sat in the yard with the dying flowers and worn prayer flags and wondered if her spirit floated near, if she felt sorrow or relief or nothing at all.

𓅩 𓅩 𓅩 𓅩

Walking home from the afternoon meeting, I passed a man struggling with a shopping cart that overflowed with cans and bottles he was collecting for cash. The wheel of the cart caught in the crack of the sidewalk just as I began to pass him. The man shouted, "Fuck you, you fucking cunt, I'm going to kill someone." I stood very still, not passing but waiting. I wanted to tell him to shut up, keep quiet, to insult him. But a headline flashed through my mind:

WOMAN BLUDGEONED TO DEATH BY LOCAL
BOTTLE COLLECTOR FOR UNTIMELY REMARKS

I passed by. A woman standing in the doorway of her home called out: "Was he saying that to you?"

I shook my head no and hurried on.

At the corner, I turned and passed a young man with a cell phone in his hand. He looked up at me and said hello. A woman with a baby nodded to me as she bent over to tuck a blanket around the child. I stopped at the next corner and looked down the street at the vigil. People stood, leaning into each other, in front of Kathleen's house. Heads bowed, hands clasped or resting on each other's shoulders. They looked like a single swaying mass. I crossed the street, walked away.

———

I imagine a man breaking into her home. He breaks the glass of the back door and it tinkles to the floor. Kathleen is boiling tea water. Kathleen is in her bed. Kathleen is in her favorite chair with a book whose pages fall easily open. She isn't afraid. "Who's there?" she calls, thinking it's the wind. She is afraid. "Who is it?"

She gives him her car keys, her wallet, all her valuables; she was not a person to care about possessions. She holds her pup in her arms, calming its bark.

She tries to reason with him. She fights back. She hits hard. She screams. She runs.

෴ ෴ ෴ ෴

We wonder what the final moments will be like: our loved ones at our side, holding our hands, watching as our last breaths slip away, opening the window to let our souls free. We imagine we have a lease on life, that our life is our own.

Louise Erdrich wrote: *Your life feels different on you, once you greet death and understand your heart's position.*

I find this printed at the bottom of my daily planner, on Sunday, October 24, United Nation's Day, as I am writing things in my weekly schedule. A list of things to do that keeps me safe from the unexpected and inexplicable.

You wear your life like a garment from the mission bundle sale ever after—

Was there a moment before Kathleen lost consciousness that she thought of anything other than her survival?

Lightly because you realize you never paid nothing for it, cherishing because you know you won't ever come by such a bargain again. Erdrich finishes.

Kathleen goes to the door after the knock. He forces himself in. *What do you want? Why are you here? Please, take what you want.* Does she know him? Kathleen goes to the door after the knock. She happily lets him in and offers him tea.

Kathleen goes to the door after the knock.

"I try to protect myself," one woman in the meeting said. "Lock the doors, say my prayers."

A man speaks, "I know I don't understand, being a man and all, how it feels to be a woman, afraid." This is said as though women are biologically fearful. Or perhaps because of their maternal instincts (the instinct to nurture others?) they are more fearful. Am I more fearful?

Ten days have passed since the murder. In the kitchen, I ask my husband how he feels. "Sad," he says.

"Are you afraid?" I say.

"No."

"Why? Because you think you can beat a guy even if he's got a gun?"

"Yes," he says and laughs lightly.

I sit at the kitchen counter while he fixes soup and sandwiches for dinner.

"I don't understand why you aren't afraid. Are you afraid for me?" I ask.

"Yes, I am always afraid for you though."

"Don't you find that awful?"

"I guess."

———

I imagine the inside of Kathleen's home: the walls are painted—
red, yellow, green. Posters hang, "Make Art Not War," and there
are framed photographs of the people she loved—her son, her
mother, a sister, a friend. A shelf of beautiful books she planned
to read just as soon as winter set in and a smooth stone she found
on a trip to the ocean with a lover she had not wanted to let go but
did. The curtains are light and airy, meant to let in as much sun as
possible. Her dishes are handmade or secondhand. A bowl on the
floor is half-filled with water for the dog. A square of fabric hangs
over the old television she uses for watching movies. Dried flowers in a vase on the kitchen counter from her summer garden remind her of a day she watched the shadows of leaves dance on the
fence and felt something akin to salvation.

༉ ༉ ༉ ༉

After twelve days, the news releases a photo of a man in a car from
an ATM camera. Some sources say the man was in Kathleen's car,
using Kathleen's card. The police only say that they believe this
man has significant information about her death.

The man looks young, like a woman. He has light hair and skin, a
sharp nose and jaw.

I walk on the sidewalk, toward home. The day is cool and the
leaves have turned. I search the yards for places I would've liked to
occupy as a child. Little corners with intricacies were best for play.
I loved small spaces. The light shines into a yard with a gooseberry bush. I see a corner under a window where the grass meets
the side of the house—the lawn is neatly kept. I imagine what I'd
bring there. A tea set, dolls, paper and crayons, an old magazine of
my mother's. I would pretend to be someone else: a different girl
who lived in a different world, with her same family, only I would
have a maid, and we'd all wear pretty, old-fashioned dresses. My
hair would be curled like Pollyanna's.

As a child, I never worried. But my mother must have, my father too. They raised five girls. "Men are animals," my father once told me. I looked away. I suppose I believed him, or at least I understood the implications of his statement—he wanted to scare me into caution. Fear, he believed, could protect me, but at what cost? Later, when I moved away, he sent me mace along with a box of chocolates and a small stuffed bear for Valentine's Day. I still have the bear.

🐦 🐦 🐦 🐦

Did Kathleen lie on the floor in blood, dying? What did she think about?

I want to believe we know that our final moment is our last. That we can somehow harness this closing breath and collect it all, every last ounce of it, and this will be enough because it must.

I want to believe, and so I make believe. I imagine she remembered her son as a boy, his laughter. I imagine the sun glistening over a field of timothy grass where she stands. Her son crouches down in the field, hiding. She walks toward him, the wind rustles the grass—she can hear the sound, she can feel the sun warm on her young face. *I'm coming*, she calls. And he laughs. He is five years old. She sees him stand and turn, his face with its smile lighting across it. He runs toward her and then he is in her arms and all she can feel is her heart pounding against this small body, this boy, this love. Shutting her eyes, only this memory survives.

The news says the man in the photograph is no longer a suspect. They've found Kathleen's car abandoned in the woods sixty miles away. The news reports that the man in the photo was actually Kathleen. There was a break-in at the Snow Bowl, a ski mountain close to the abandoned car—they believe it to be her murderer.

———————

Is it true that I am more fearful because I am a woman? I am more fearful now, but a woman was murdered. I try to explain to my husband that when a woman is harmed, other women feel as though they too have been harmed. There exists an intimacy between women that has to do with the violence they experience. He looks up from his soup to catch my watchful eye. "You identify with her?" he asks.

But I don't respond.

There is no sign of forced entry, the police report. There was a struggle inside. We hoped for something quick, an accident. But this was not the case.

❧ ❧ ❧ ❧

Last night my husband and I drove by Kathleen's, and dozens of candles were lit at the shrine. No one was there; no one wants to be out after dark now. The glow of the candles looked serene, peaceful. Someone hung prayer flags from the corner of the house to the tent of the shrine and they waved in the little breeze over the sidewalk. "Look at all the prayers," I said, too quiet for my husband to hear.

Don't we deserve to enter and occupy the gap that closes between this world and the next? I want to believe in her final moment. I want to believe there is some thought, attuned to grace, that arose. At least if we are going to be killed we will be given this—a final thought, a last light. But isn't the point more that we deserve safety? We deserve not to be harmed—no final moment of reprieve could erase what was done to her.

A man at the meeting falls asleep and starts snoring. No one cares or bothers waking him up. "I pray about fear," someone says. "I know some fear is irrational." I stare at the clock, irritated. I don't care how much I disagree with what they are saying, I feel like we all need to hold each other's arms and walk in a long line around the town shouting, crying, chanting. I fantasize about something happening, some sort of change. I see a bulbous cloud drifting out over the lake. Across the way the trees flame red, orange, yellow in the light of autumn.

A friend tells me that Tibetan prayer flags do not send prayers to the gods for the individual. But in fact, the mantras written on each flag send good will and harmony to all. The wind carries their sacred hopes all over the world without prudence for who deserves a better life, compassion, good fortune, prosperity, health, or luck.

The police report that they have a man in custody and are certain he's the killer. They found him hiding in a shed on top of a mountain at the Snow Bowl ski resort. He'd been googling Kathleen's name on his laptop for the past three days. People say he was a friend of hers, though perhaps estranged.

༺༻

A month has passed, and I have stopped attending the community meetings. I walk home alone one day, wearing my life like a loose garment, thinking about the bargain we've all received. I pull the garment in different directions to fit my body. I yank on it and a string comes loose. I sit in the grass near the gooseberry bush in the yard that I would have liked as a child and sew the garment back. I wonder who will go next and how close she will be—will she be me? Alone in the house I hear noises. I avoid the basement, check the closets, look under the bed.

I go out in the rain with my red umbrella and walk the side streets toward Kathleen's. The leaves stick to the pavement and I know when they dry and blow away they'll leave their outline in the sidewalk for a couple of days. I wonder if the big elm by the church with the many Jesus Christs will bloom orange then red like a fire going out in the night.

At the stoop, a cup of cappuccino in a saucer, a tiny notebook with a miniature pen attached to it sits under the eaves, out of the rain. I touch my wet finger to the thin rim of the cup: it's cold. When I stand up my scarf blows free in the wind; I wrap it snuggly around my neck. Under the tent a few candles burn among dozens of objects left like offerings. A plastic toy spider catches my eye and I pick it up. For a moment, I want to dance it along a branch or make it crawl over the copper Buddha . . . to sing a little tune. Instead I get down on my knees and start to pray. *Please, please, please* is all that comes.

On the Life of Objects

A piece of yarn coils over the egg-shaped stone on the window-sill of the bedroom. We collected rocks as children. Sold them at our store along with braided grass necklaces, friendship bracelets made of colored string, and once a sunfish caught from the lake. I collect stones from the places I go when I'm away from home. I keep them in cloth pouches, wooden boxes, on the sills of windows, the kitchen counter, the rim of the bath. Smooth stones are best: the eye lingers with pleasure on the surface. Porous rocks, rocks with holes from the sea, from creatures, from magic, scare me. I do not like to swim in places where I cannot see the bottom. But, I will. I do not like to look at surfaces that lack congruity of shape and surface.

I discover postcards sent years ago from a friend: a picture of the manger scene, of Beijing nightlife, and of mountains. I like to think of the distance traveled by these rectangles of stock paper, some glossy, some matte. The words swirl and bound with the echo of an unfamiliar place: *dog shit collects in the streets of Kraków, the men here are all shorter than me, pigeons in every city.* No one sends postcards anymore.

As children, we pressed autumn leaves between wax paper with my mother. I still find her wildflowers flattened between the pages of heavy books. My mother does not collect things, though, like me, she finds meaning in objects. Her jewelry boxes are messy, always missing earrings, silver chains knotted, unwearable. Sometimes I have found small rocks there that she must have absent-mindedly slipped into her pocket. She would have found them months later, not remembering where they'd come from, laying them among the disarray of her accessories, or remembering, she placed them like treasure in her box of jewels.

A tiny vase filled with stone, birch bark, dried heather, and sage ash sits beside a wooden bird bending toward the ground, legs of wire mounted on carved wood, painted brown.

My grandfather's war photos, the newspaper clippings he kept. I touch these objects and think of how he touched them too. A picture from the war of an old Korean woman with her hands in prayer, on the back, in my grandfather's hand, "woman begging for a smoke." Is it meant to be funny or sad? I don't believe she was begging for a smoke. I am suspicious of my grandfather's interpretation. But perhaps she was.

What exists in objects that draw us to them? What powers do they hold? My favorite childhood book was about a donkey that turned into a stone. It involved a tiny red wishing pebble, a hungry lion in the woods, a sudden wish of panic: Make me a stone! When the winter snow fell on the donkey-turned-stone, I always felt sad for him—how awful to be so alone. All things could feel the pang of loneliness in my childhood mind.

History is filled with missing objects. Seeking lost objects sets history's plot, the journey, and its end: found object. Objects solve mysteries, illuminate crimes, reveal guilt; objects ward off evil, protect, and destroy. Objects promise love: rings exchanged or gifts bestowed.

My husband collects baseball cards and toy figurines. This he does compulsively, lovingly, expectant. He likes to set these objects in order: to stack the cards into piles, to line up the figurines that he, alone, will view. These objects are not for sharing, though on occasion, when children visit, he allows them to play with certain figurines. I used to get annoyed with him for wasting money on his collections. Though baseball cards might turn a profit one day, this is not his intention. The collecting of objects provides a sense of safety, along with the pleasure of more and yet never enough. Collecting wards off ending. His objects refuse to let the past slink away, to let childhood dim into remnants of something lost.

I gave my sister Hannah a Celtic cross for a graduation gift. She lost it in the woods near the sauna at our grandparents' cabin at Burnt Shanty Lake. Sometimes we still look for it. My mother lost her wedding diamond while cleaning the toilet; my father lost his wedding band because he never wore it. Last he saw it hanging with a safety pin from the green leaf of a houseplant. He had put it there for safekeeping during a move.

We do not worry about the lost objects that represent living bonds we feel remain intact; though, should we doubt our marriage, our friendship, our sisterhood, we worry losing an object of sentiment might be a bad omen.

❧❧❧❧

Late October, a friend and I are walking through the flower garden and picking what is left of the crop. I ask her about the life of objects. We bend low over the black-eyed Susans—she with the clippers, me with can.

"What objects?" she asks.

"Not useful ones like a toothbrush or spoon," I say.

We are clipping flowers to bring to a memorial outside a woman's home. Amazed that anything still survives, my friend calls to me each time she finds a pretty bloom. I walk down the row. We make flowers into objects by cutting. I have never learned the names of flowers except those my mother taught me as a girl. In her book of flowers, my mother writes the date and location of each flower seen. Sometimes I flip through it and read her entries:

Common Blue Iris—*first spring flower in front of our cabin, 1981*
Bull Thistle—*In the berry patch, July 1987*
Joe-Pye-Weed—*Beatrice Lake shortcut, '85, '86*
Wild Columbine—*Dad's cabin*
Spotted Touch-Me-Nots—*by the lake at Burnt Shanty*
Common Pansy—*Sand pit on a berry hunt right before it rained,*
  July 1987

I always look for the oldest date, but why? Time has its talons in me.

The October sky is luscious, gorged and wrapped in thick cloud, colored and dreamlike, deep and lonely. The sky is not object. Does the sky object? My friend says, "Objects are symbolic, they give meaning; so, even the objects that don't seem to have a purpose, have one, if they bring meaning to our life. Meaning is a purpose." Is it?

The wind and chill of fall pinks our cheeks, and I am thankful for this feeling of cold and the heat of my body. "It's too complex," I say, "then you have to think about language, animals don't have objects for meaning." The magic inside of my mind utterly fails in translation.

We walk on. The fall colors are at peak brilliance right now. I love traversing this farmland in the place we call the Intervale: the low land between the Winooski River and Lake Champlain. I want to photograph this day but none of the pictures I've taken of moments that filled me with longing and seeing ever captured that. The pictures I love are those of accidental genius, happenstance: Hannah and I beside a glacial lake, aqua blue in the sunlight, my hands lift to hold back my wind-tossed hair and she crosses her arms, squints, frowns. Her blond hair is lit with sunlight. It captures the essence of who we were in that moment—eighteen and sixteen—angry, bemused, yet so sure of ourselves, so certain of the way life would go.

Is it simply that objects remind us, remember, hold symbolic something other than what they are? Do we use objects like language, to represent what is absent? The woman who owns the house we live in left three smooth stones along the windowsill in the bedroom as though keeping watch. Her stones fill me with a sense of calm, a pleasure in the presence of the outer world within. They mean something to me, but not perhaps what they had meant to her. Where are they from? Do they mark a special place, a certain day, a beloved person?

I have entered many homes filled with the world of nature: rocks, stones, leaves, sticks, dried flowers, antlers, a bird's nest. I feel instantly at home. Sentimental objects like ceramic cats will never do. When I sit in a room filled with knickknacks, I am estranged, dislocated, filled with remorse. But should someone tack a slice of birch bark, frayed and curling pink, to the wall, I feel comforted. I confess birch trees occupied much of the landscape of my childhood, and in my memory, birch shoot up and thrive.

🐾 🐾 🐾 🐾

A memorial raised outside the house where a woman was murdered consists of objects. Flowers, plastic butterflies, prayer flags, a stuffed animal, a cup of coffee, a tin with a piece of Wrigley's Spearmint gum and a square of dark chocolate, crosses, notes, pictures of the woman in her garden smiling. My friend and I bend down to sit on the wool blanket someone has left for kneeling. We look at the collection of objects. She places our can of flowers among them. The objects distract us from thinking or speaking. They remind us of the woman when she was still alive.

My friend and I stand in the backyard of the woman's house. We should not be here, really. "Do you think she is still here?" I ask. My friend stays quiet, sensing.

"Yes, she's here, she's going to be here for a little while, I think," she says with a confidence that startles me.

Objects exist in collusion with the past—calling it back, forcing reentry. There was once comfort in walking through my grandparents' homes, knowing that the place of things remained unchanged. My own parents won't stop rearranging their home— objects appear and disappear, some never return. Sofas change location based on the season, tables are moved, hutches switch corners, and one of my childhood bedrooms no longer exists, its walls were torn down and removed. I have inherited this compulsion to transform and change the rooms of my own home, season after season. Objects become extensions of us. They sit like lost appendages on the shelves of our homes—the other selves, the ones we tried on and discarded, are often there in the shadows. Behind the glass doors of a hutch I've long owned, I hide a pair of wooden angels given as gifts. They mark loss and though I don't display them, I can't let them go.

Some objects we keep hidden but can't abolish. Every time I move I'm forced to deal with them. Many of mine are sentimental gifts like books meant to inspire. Anything trying to inspire me fails. I want to banish these objects from my kingdom but my girlhood self is still very much alive in me—she worries over these orphans, begs me not to let them go.

Once, as a child on an open-window trolley through the forest, I stood beside my mother. She held Bess, my baby sister at the time, in her arms. My sister held a teddy bear. It might have been Tennessee, or some state near West Virginia, where we lived at the time. We were on a day trip seeing autumn. The woods lay below in a ravine, colored of fall, far off, away. The bear slipped from the hands of my sister, through the window. And though my mother reached out to save the bear, it tumbled down and was gone. My sister was not old enough to understand her loss. She clapped her hands together; she had tiny eyes and white-blond curls. This began my wishing and imagining game, which would continue into adulthood.

How I imagined that bear! Toppled down into a forest, dark and misty. Sad, the bear, lost, the bear. I wished, imagined, over and over, silently, never aloud—as though I knew the triviality of my game—my hand reaching out, just as the bear slipped, clasping on, saving the bear. Mother, thankful. Good. Sometime later, in my bed at night, in the dark, I wished for the bear. If only I could set him upright, against a tree, he would feel less awful about being lost. If I could tell him it was an accidental loss. He was not a lost object to me then.

ᘛ ᘛ ᘚ ᘚ

I prefer the life of objects remain secret and giddy. I prefer the mystery of things. I like to remember the childhood objects so well loved by my sisters and me. A red purse Hannah once filled with army worms, a cheap jewelry box with a spinning ballerina that required winding, a scrap of baby blanket my sister still sleeps with at age twenty-nine, stones, leaves, sticks, braided grass, and birch bark. They enter and retreat, sometimes laughing, sometimes silent. I admit to giving them human qualities like laughter and sorrow.

I fantasize about the life of so-called *useless* objects. The stone with yarn coiled round sits, and I suppose it is true it reminds me, calls meaning to me. I made the yarn on a windy fall day at a farm where I worked. The stone is not mine, nor really is this piece of yarn made of sheep's wool and dye, of fingers twisting, fingers holding the twist, of fingers letting loose. Objects are the antithesis to letting go. "No," they call out, "sit with, let be, remain."

Looking at a Photograph
of a Deer Head

A bit of crusted snow catches on clumps of grass in a field. I can hear it crunch underfoot. The sky is a whitewash in the foreground. Then a flimsy wire fence, perhaps the entrance to an orchard or pasture. At the center of the photo stands Andrea Modica's subject: the trunk of a tree with one skinny naked bough caught by the camera lens, and then, hanging from a rope, the severed head of a deer—upright as though its body would soon join the head in leaping over the fence across the field into the ashen white unknown. I imagine the deer running free from the rope, a swish of white fading into the washed-out sky.

I discovered Modica's work during a time of mourning in my life when the loss of my first pregnancy felt crippling. Her photographs, devoid of all things quaint or sentimental, relayed a stark honesty that comforted me: the truth of not turning away, of looking. She casts death and ending in all her work. Her subjects often carry this weight: bones, clipped hair, animal skulls, the blurred image of an obese child, bodies tangled in sullen embrace, a dead bird. And what great art doesn't nurse death, court eternity? It's different though with her photographs. They reveal another way of seeing, teach to look again, but never answer the question of how or why or what for. Rather, Modica asks the viewer to answer her own question. The one that gathers in her as she looks.

As a child, I examined the head of a stuffed deer mounted in the hallway at my grandparents' lake cabin in northern Minnesota. I felt the rough catch of its fur and the smooth black skin of its nose.

Marble eyed, the deer looked everywhere and nowhere. Sometimes, after dark, it scared me. I'd run down the hallway to pass
it and leap into the big bed where I slept with my three sisters. But
in daylight, uncloaked of its powers, it no longer made me run. Instead, I imagined that its body stood on the other side of the wall
and that it was just poking its head in to say hello.

The summer I was eleven, my grandfather slept in the bedroom
at the end of the hallway, rather than on the couch in the living
room. The deer head had been removed. He died on a sunny afternoon, his wife and children beside him. The sounds of his grandchildren laughing and playing in the lake drifted in through the
open window. Life had leaked out of him, until there was nothing
left but the end.

Later, I watched the men from the morgue carry his body away
in a black bag. I stood at the end of the hallway as they took him
out the back door. It comforted me to watch the removal of death
from life. How easily he was zipped in and taken away. Yet it
seemed to me, as a child, that something of him remained like a
light and airy shadow at the edge of the forest, or in the smudged
halo of the moon as I walked through the summer grass. Perhaps
it was only my imagination. The years passed into decades.

Still, I imagine his ghost sleeps through winter beneath the
snow that coats the cabin like fur. In the spring, he wanders the
woods, lingering like smoke. Waiting for our return, he notices
the green buds of birch; he smells the rich scent of mud and longs
for a cigarette. We stayed away longer and longer, until eventually, we never returned. Now I wonder how he passes the days.
I see him sitting on the hill overlooking the lake, a can of beer in
one hand, a lit cigarette in the other. He sets the beer in the grass
and swipes a hand through his thinning gray hair. He waves to
his friend Hysh, also a schoolteacher, who is out swimming in the
bay. I see him rambling, like a sleepy Pan, down forest paths to the
point, our old fort, where he might lay on a bed of moss to rest. I
see him standing in the lake, waist-deep, looking out at the quiet
of dusk. I see him smoking on the deck, long limbed and laughing,

as he tells me, "You can go swimming, but you can't get wet," his
favorite joke.

Looking at Modica's photograph, I imagine a young boy as hunter.
His hair dark and shoulders narrow, a phantom, like my own lost
child. The deer, his first kill. He slit open the body, careful not to
nick the gut or intestines. I imagine the inner organs spilling onto
the cold snow, steaming, and the warm rivers of blood staining the
ground red. Was it beautiful or terrifying or merely a simple act of
necessity? Or was it (most likely) a ritual passing into manhood?
And why did he leave the deer head hanging in its noose—an act
of pride or imagination?

I am not sad about the deer head any more than I am sad about
Grandfather. The myth of my grandfather remains that of death.
First death, much like the first taste of dirt and blood in your
mouth, shocks. I stomped my foot. I folded my skinny arms across
my chest and demanded to know where he had gone. Heaven, my
mother said. But he felt too close for that.

Did the boy feel life dissipate, feel the quiver of the end when
the steam rose and the blood pooled? Did the soul of the deer escape into the earth, the air, the ether? Or did it join, as some believe, the body of the boy?

On windy nights in those parts—the gray world of Modica's
lens—the boy moves through the woods, silent as a doe, his body
quick and lean, his breath rising like a quiet fog. He follows the
path to the field where the sky is washed out, ashen gray, and fe-
vered. And when he sees the head of the deer, he begins to run until he reaches the wiry fence, pulls open the gate, and disappears.
Where, I wonder, has he gone?

Laughing Water

The Game

By mid-August, my mother, brother, and I spend our last days together lounging beside the lake. They will return to school in a couple of weeks—she as a student counselor and he as a high school junior—and I'll go back to Vermont and my husband, who has already left to start his job at a school. With summer on the wane, we've abandoned all projects and productive activities, anxious to relish these last days. The sisters who live nearby and our father sometimes join us. Usually, we're alone. The air begins to turn, the sun's heat softens. Water laps against the beach, and I think of Aden as a little boy making moats in the sand. Then my brother says, "River." I look at him and nod, "Fountain." We turn to my mother, who lays her book in her lap, looks out over the lake, "Youth." And the game begins.

You can play the game anywhere . . . standing in line at the grocery store, waiting for a table at the local grill, or here on the dock. It takes almost no effort except your attention, which is what my brother's after. It's his game, his way of pulling his sisters and mother from their books and daydreams into his world. One person says a word and the next person says the first word that comes to mind when hearing that word. Aden says, "Cartoon," Mom says, "Character," I say, "Book," Aden says, "Lost Boys," Mom says, "Sudan," I say, "Honda." And so it goes, round after round until one of us tires.

Later, I lie on my belly at the end of the dock, dipping my fingers into the shallow water. It's a small lake. You can see the other side. Our end, the shallow side, made of a long stretch of yellow sand beach, faces west and the setting sun.

I watch them put on snorkel goggles and swim out past the reeds. They dive under searching for lost objects—a tin can, a glass bottle, some shiny remnant of the past. When they come up for a break, Mom's body looks narrow, dwarfed compared to my brother's. She is small like a cat, I think. My brother, still unused to the breadth of his own shoulders, the height of his new body, lunges into her. She sinks down with him, the strap of her goggles breaking loose. I hear them shouting, then my brother's laugh. I wonder if my mother senses the ephemeral nature of this moment.

Mom holds her goggles to her face with both hands, kicking hard to make up for the lost motion of her arms. My brother surfaces, holding something shiny in his hand. He shouts and my mother comes up too. The sun glistens on their wet skin and hair as they examine the shiny object, only momentarily, because in truth, what they're looking for isn't yet lost.

Lost

Five years ago, the summer I met him, my husband and I spent nights at the beach on Lake Champlain in Vermont. The night water, a liquid universe unlike the lake of daylight, emitted a clandestine aura ideal for new love. I had just moved to Vermont, running as I always was back then, away from myself. I worked for my cousin at his coffeehouse. Josh worked at the burrito shop next door. He would not be my husband for another five years. I don't know that we believed such a future existed for us that first summer together. He'd come into the coffeehouse at the end of my shift and wipe the tables for me while I closed out the till. He stood beside me as I locked the door, then we'd dash for his car, a teal

Dodge Shadow he called Minnehaha, after the fictional American Indian woman whose name is connected to parks and creeks and schools and waterfalls in Minnesota, my home. It seemed odd that he was familiar with the name. When I asked him about it, he cited the Longfellow poem *The Song of Hiawatha*, where she was first created. "Minnehaha," he told me, "means laughing water."

From the gravel parking lot, we walked across a soccer field, through a patch of woods, onto a bike path, and then down the wooden steps to the beach. At the edge of the soccer field, he'd pause and take my hand, whispering, "Watch out for the rock in the path, remember, it's a little to the left." I always forgot the rock. The size of a large dog, it was easy to bump into. The way he held my hand then, came from a need to hold on to me. He felt like I was only drifting through, fleeting, enough that he'd stay out half the night with me though he worked early the next morning and never seemed to grow tired. And he was right, I never wanted to hold on to anyone for long.

We tore our clothes off on shore and ran in. The water was shallow a far distance out; I would sometimes hide from him in the shadows of the lake. I'd make him turn away, close his eyes, count . . . then I would quietly swim off. There was nothing to hide behind or in but shadow, so I floated on my back with only my lips and nose rising from the surface of the lake, waiting.

One August night he seemed to really lose me. Even with my head above water, the tops of my shoulders in the breeze, he couldn't see me. There was no moon. I heard him grow quiet, move away, and then a silence. He too was lost in the dark.

Night after night we swam there. Alone, together in the moonlight, with a bay of clouds drifting fast, reminding me of time and then antitime—fleeting hope that we could devolve time, that the night would remain, and we would never have to face what waited on the other side of the sky.

A single sailboat anchored off the point of land that curved out to the south created half a cove. We imagined we would learn to sail together. We'd buy a boat, go down the Atlantic Coast all the way to the islands of the Caribbean, or maybe we'd live in a tiny cabin on the shore of Lake Champlain and sail this lake. Either option seemed equally as impossible as possible at the time. But, then, we were always dreaming of a future that embodied the two of us. Believing that if we kept imagining a future together it might fill the uncertainty of now just enough to keep us there.

Uncertainty

At night, in my bedroom at my parents' house in Minnesota, I hear the sound of a basketball on the pavement in the driveway. It's dark, but there's a light in the driveway where my brother practices shooting. *Dribble, dribble, pause, bounce* is a comforting sound, but one that reminds me he leads an inner life that I'll never know, lives out spaces of solitude, finds devotion a form of pleasure.

My brother told us this summer that he wants to go to northern Idaho for college. There's a town there, he says, with a lake and mountains. Coeur d'Alene. That's the name. He, our sister Bess, and our parents stopped in this town on their way to Washington State during the camping trip they took this summer. He tells me he plans to major in business then become a lawyer. Mom doesn't believe he's serious about moving so far away in just two years; she can't yet imagine his absence in any way. He is her last child, her only son, and she still makes him lunch. He tells her jokingly it's her job. Yet next month he'll be seventeen. "Maybe," he tells us, "I'll just work for the Department of Natural Resources, that way I won't have to drive into town to go to work." My family prefers to sequester themselves sixteen miles north of town, in the woods beside a small lake, in the log house Dad built twenty years ago. Sometimes I feel like I belong to a small tribe. Going to town, especially in the summer, is to be avoided, particularly by our mother, who has her summers off. "Good idea," I say, wanting to encourage something perhaps inspired by passion and not financial gain alone. But I know that he will need to put distance between himself and the clan soon enough.

Distance

We are not alike this way: at his age, I wanted to get as far away from my parents as possible; their control over me felt stifling. I wanted to spend every weekend at parties with my friends or on road trips to concerts in Minneapolis or Duluth. My father and I fought bitterly over the boundaries of his control, the limits of my freedom. I suppose he knew the risks I took: the drunk driving, the parties, the recklessness. At least, I want to believe this. I want to believe his desire to protect me was boundless. We would stand in the kitchen arguing with each other about what I was doing Saturday night. His face stilled, his arms folded across his chest, "You're not doing that," he'd say.

"Why? I can't believe you're doing this to me."

"You're just not."

"I hate you. You know that, I really hate you."

But my father also cried the day after I came home drunk at fifteen. My mother was the angry one then. My father sat on my sister's bed and started to cry for me, for the loss he knew was inevitable and the sorrow of what I must learn. *Please don't do this to yourself,* I hear him saying, but those weren't exactly his words. The history of alcoholism in our family must have loomed in his mind, but not yet my own. And here is the point: my brother is nothing like this. There is nothing dangerous hidden in his midst, he does not openly disobey the rules or scream at my father; I doubt he's ever told someone he hates them.

———————

Though Aden says he'll go to Idaho, he's a homebody and spends most weekend evenings watching sports on television or shooting hoops in the driveway. I remember him most as a small and cuddly child, who liked to sit on his sisters' laps, who loved cross-country road trips because the eight of us were finally together for long stretches of time in the family minivan or suburban. I was thirteen when he was born, so by the time he was there it was rare that we were all together. I remember his tiny hands, the wrists and palms scarred from burns and skin grafting. I remember how carefully I held onto them.

Fears

When Aden was around eleven months old he fell against the side of a wood-burning stove in our cabin on Burnt Shanty Lake. It must have been a chilly summer morning, my mother was in the next room, her back turned for a minute, and my brother, just learning to walk, fell. He put out his hands to catch himself against the side of the pot-bellied iron stove, which was hot. Stunned and lacking balance, he didn't push away at first. My sister Hannah remembers the smell of his singed skin, similar to that of burned scrambled eggs. He was badly hurt. They took skin from the back of one of his thighs and grafted it on each wrist. Today his wrists and palms are still scarred, but because I don't want him to catch me looking at them, don't want to make him self-conscious of this small imperfection, I have never been able to form a picture of what his palms and wrists really look like.

A year ago this summer, he had another surgery because of a lack of range and mobility in his thumbs—his hands don't open as much as they should. When this happened, my brother was forced to change his shot, which continues to plague his ability to score, particularly three-pointers, on the court. He needs to score threes because, like my father, he's a point guard and not tall enough to play down low, and point guards need to score threes. Last night I heard the sound of the ball on the court out back and I could tell from the rhythm that my dad was rebounding for him. Though Aden would never say that he has lost his touch, this seems to be a growing fear within the family. When I ask my father, himself a lifelong ball player, about Aden's shot, he mostly shrugs off the question but once said, "Oh, geez, I don't know if it'll ever get better." A nervous worry in his voice. Tonight, Aden's alone shooting hoops in the driveway. I think of the loneliness of devotion, the drive and desire that must exist in him. But also, the complete abandon of passion.

Lonely

I remembered the dark of that night five years ago, in the midst of our game of hide and seek, when the moon lifted over the trees of the southern shore of Lake Champlain. I saw Josh standing, the water up to his belly, alone, with his back to me. I couldn't see his face, but I could tell from the slouch of his shoulders, his fingers drifting along the surface of the lake, that he was lonely. I, a lonely person myself, a person who sought to externalize her loneliness by moving to a new state, felt in communion.

It was not until the fall of our first-year dating that I returned to the night swimming cove in the daylight. Riding my bike out along the bike path that followed the shore of the lake north, I stopped, locked up my bike, and walked down the wooden steps to the beach. Maybe it was just the wrong time of year, but the water, a murky sea-green color, was littered with trash, the shore lined with empty beer cans and bottles. I stood alone looking out at the place on the lake where the sailboat was once anchored and wondered if it had really been here that I had fallen in love.

Home

At the end of that first summer of dating Josh, I returned home to Minnesota. My family took me to their new cabin on a tiny island, less than an acre in size, in Lake Vermilion near the Boundary Waters Canoe Area. At the cabin, my brother, then eleven, and I sat alone on the deck beside the lake, watching the moon drift low in the sky, making a puddle of white light on the lake.

"Aden," I said, "do you think there are people who live out there?" I nodded at the moon, a single upward swoop of my chin.

"No," he said.

"What, why not?" I thought a child would want to imagine other planets, other places, and people.

"God would tell us if there were."

"Really, how?" I looked down at him. He was just a little boy.

"He'd write it in the Bible."

I was quiet then, crushed that my parents would teach him this. Did they teach him this? I try to imagine my father telling his only son that everything about the world is written in this one book. Of course he wouldn't. But I still resented the way their religion crowded me with fear that I wasn't good enough the way I am, that my desires were wrong, and that the Lord would punish me for it. I feared that this religion would turn my brother against me. I could not think of anything else to say. In our mutual silence, I felt a part of me closing.

The first years I dated my husband I kept this part of me closed. It seems so stupid and cliché to say *I would not let him in*; I would not let him close. It is a sort of love paradigm—the come here, go away. But love was not fearless in my family home, it was something I felt could easily humiliate or even destroy me. I kept him at a distance in the usual ways: criticism, fighting, withholding my affections. He stayed and when he finally realized the depth of my vulnerability, he was astounded. Perhaps it was an accident, or I had just grown tired, but somehow, he discovered—much to my horror—how deeply wounded I was. He never said just how he'd uncovered the truth—it seems silly, now, but it wasn't then. I remember the day, the hour of dusk, light through the yellow curtains, when he said, "You tricked me, Emily."

I could tell he was serious, a rare state for him. "What. Why?" Perhaps we'd been dating a year or more.

"You made me believe that you weren't vulnerable, that you were a rock."

"What do you mean?" It felt like he was retelling me a story he'd invented.

"It's terrifying to see how vulnerable you are, how weak."

It hurt my feelings.

Later I would say, "But we are all wounded, but we are all vulnerable."

To which he replied, "I could never see it in you."

I don't know such a person. I don't recognize her, the one he named. But when he left, years after discovering the vulnerable me, I realized that it was her, the one who wanted invincibility, that made him go.

At night in my bedroom at the end of August in Minnesota, I listen to the pounding of the basketball. At the pause, I fill in the sound "swoosh." My brother, even at sixteen, when kids are supposed to be filled with teenage angst, spends most of his evenings at home with us.

When I leave at the end of August, my brother comes out to the driveway, along with my sister and my mother, to say goodbye. He calls us into a group hug that feels like a huddle. We hold on to each other for a long time, pretending like he's a small child we want to please, though of course he's not. This is his gift to us—this openness, this show of affection that he has always been able to orchestrate between us. The dog jumps up and my brother laughs, delighted. As the youngest, he has always been hard pressed to have his whole family with him at the same time. He was five when I first left home for college in Minneapolis.

Leave

Josh tells me that whenever I leave Minnesota for Vermont, exchanging one life for the other, which I do every summer and Christmas, I mourn the lost life for a time. Today, my first day back in Vermont, I lie on the bed in our new home, crying. I move back and forth between my childhood home in Minnesota and my current life in Vermont as if lingering between lives. But I can't imagine another way. Minnesota eventually grows heavy. I feel inhibited by the life of my family: their expectations of success or definitions of it, which are not mine, begin to erode my sometimes-tenuous selfhood. Mental regression takes hold of me when I return home—the wild creature that I cultivate in Vermont crumbles under scrutiny in Minnesota. Yet, Minnesota offers solace of its own—its lakes and forests a haven in their own right.

I lie on the bed in our new home, which isn't really our new home, but the master bedroom of an old mismatched house a friend lets us occupy while the owner is away. The upstairs rooms are painted pale blue, green, and yellow colors as though expecting multiple babies, while the downstairs rooms are mismatched relics of the past: the wallpaper in the kitchen a tacky orange and pea green from the sixties, the blue trim of the piano room outmoded, and the hat and flower basket paper in the living room a comical vision of an unidentifiable era. But the stones collected from the lake or streams, laid along the edge of the bathtub and on the windowsills, make me feel at home.

I tell Josh I am crying because the trees in the yard are over a hundred years old. Those trees, the tall ones with worlds of branches drowning out the sky, take so long to grow that I will never in my life be able to plant a tree and see it grow to an age of such greatness. Somehow this causes me great pain. We lie in bed together holding hands speaking of tree kingdoms.

Kingdoms

My sister Hannah and I spent months drawing *The Kingdom of Aden*, a color-pencil picture, the size of a small window, of castles, rivers, lakes, farms, entertainment parks, trains, trails, and so on. Central to the piece was the character of the white stallion from Aden's chapter book he had written and illustrated as an eight-year-old. A month past Aden's ninth birthday, we kept at it. We both attended college in Minneapolis at the time and the nights we spent drawing and designing, coloring and shading, were given to laughter with little pressure to make serious conversation, to discuss our futures or our studies—the tests that needed studying for, the papers to be written. I imagine we drank wine out of mason jars, our hair still streaked with summer blond in October, our tans nearly gone. I imagine we laughed over the different names we came up with: Patty's Peak belonged to our mother while Tim's Tunnel named our father.

We finally gave it to him in November and it seemed to please the entire family. They all sat around one night examining the names of the places; each family member had their own landmark. But then, Hannah recalls that the drawing hung in its red frame in the entryway of the house for years. When our sister Alida's Ojibwa teacher from Minneapolis came to pick her up at the house for a ricing trip to harvest wild rice just over the Canadian border, Hannah felt embarrassed by it. The history of American land possession and the concept of "kingdom" so closely related to the colonialism that righted the destruction of millions of American Indians, a deeper wound than any of us were willing to tend.

I imagine my own kingdom to be a series of quests for love and acceptance among the many battles I staged for myself—fighting

my parents, refusing to develop a career, enrolling in the most difficult college courses in order to prove something to myself. I also
sharpened a long slow river of grief and an ocean of both sorrow
and joy, as these two feelings seem to grow from each other in me.
Here in my kingdom, a blue room, a room of smooth stones home
to a poet, a farm where I live out an entire life raising sheep and
goats, a city in a foreign language where I keep trying to gain cit-
izenship. My husband is his own destination, a place that I did not
at first discover, as it took years for us to truly find each other. My
mother is her own tall-grassed meadow. My father is a compli-
cated region, a place that since passing through my own struggles
has become again a refuge for me, though one of quietude. My
brother, I wonder, what is he? What would he be?

In a way, we all love him best. I want to say because he is easy to
love, but I don't think that easy love is strong love or best love or
well loved.

Loved

For years I couldn't remember the lines in one of Ezra Pound's
Cantos, a line that, at twenty, I was so taken with I believed it
could never leave me. Sometimes, in a library, I'd find his *Cantos*,
a tomb unto its own strange destiny. I'd sit on the floor in the aisle
flipping through it, trying to find the lines, *Was it "well loved" or
"best loved," something that stays or is kept?* They became the lost
lines I always searched for. There are things such as these lines
that in life we lose and only here and there try to recover.

Later in life, I realized that my brother was equally as sensitive as I
am when I told him that a joke he made was sexist and he responded
by screaming at me. I could feel in him a similar pain . . . close, ever
so close, to rage, an emotion marked by helplessness. I was quiet
then. I know that I am a little afraid of my love for him. Afraid that
he will quit seeing me or that he can't possibly love me as much as

his other sisters because I wasn't there and I'm still not there most of the time. I am afraid of losing him because in truth most love is limited.

During the time Josh and I were apart, before we married, I visualized us walking down the front steps of our old apartment. At the curb, we both turned and walked in different directions, growing farther and farther apart. I went home to Minnesota for a few months and spent all my time sewing a quilt of mismatched fabric. I devoted myself to that quilt. I believed in its clashing beauty. I did not tire until its completion. At night I would spread out patches on the living room floor and rearrange them, with my mother and father looking on in amusement. This was their daughter, the one they remembered as a child. She was not lost.

The things we search for only in moments of inspiration are the things we know will eventually return to us. That we instinctively know what is truly lost and what is only misplaced doesn't surprise me. There is a good portion of me that senses I already embody my entire life. That everything I need is already there in me waiting to be called forth.

I was reading a book on the craft of writing, driving in the car with my mother that July, during our summer visit, when the lost lines returned. Right there in the craft book, the author referenced the same lines:

> What thou lovest well remains,
> the rest is dross.

We passed a marsh with telephone poles and the world outside the car folded inward as the words cast me into a decade ago. As I read the lines, I felt the emotion I attached to a place in my former life—a small room where I lived one semester in terrible isolation: a sentimental truth uprooted by its reference to the eternal, confined to this small lifetime, to this small "lovest well."

Lovest Well

I understand something now that I didn't ten years ago when I first read *The Cantos*, first loved Pound (first felt crushed by his fascism, his anti-Semitism), which is that love is to be known as a verb, something we enact outwardly. Something we give that does not actually require reciprocation. An action, wordless and sound. I don't know if "the rest" is waste. But I think we all, in moments of terror over our own extinction, understand the truth of "the rest is dross."

Back on the dock in August, the dry heat of Minnesota a treasure compared to the humidity of Vermont summers, I watch the dog dozing under a shade umbrella as we play the game. Aden says, "Run," Mom says, "Fast," I say, "Lost." Aden says, "Underwear," Mom says, "Stinky," I say, "Poop." We laugh. We laugh and laugh. *Poop* will always be funny, never will it not be funny. Not *shit* or *feces*, they aren't funny, *poop*—that's a big laugh. My sister Alida shows up in long-sleeved shirt and straw hat, toting ninety block, which she starts to slather over her entire body. Aden says, "Turtle," Alida says, "Timmy," Mom says, "Tiny," I say, "Little." Aden says, "Turd," Alida says, "Poop."

Everyone gets tired of the game, but I am committed to playing it whenever my brother wants.

With my husband, I spent the first years of our dating life searching for evidence of his love, coming up empty-handed, denying its existence. I did not know how to love him, I was fearful of what such a love might do to me. It would take a year without him to learn what thou lovest well . . .

Back in Vermont, on our enormous rented bed with the trees growing well beyond the housetops, I take out my imaginary kingdom of Emily map and draw a city to be named Coeur d'Alene, which the

French translate as an insult meaning "sharp hearted." The heart of an awl, which means the heart of a tool that pierces things—a piercing heart? A name the French fur traders gave the native people of what is now called northern Idaho. In a way, I think we all need an awl for piercing our hearts. I think back to Minnehaha, which actually translates as "waterfall" and not "laughing water"—isn't the term *laughing water* much better than *waterfall*? Having marked this city with a name, I draw a line. I let it wrap around mountains, settle beside a river, I don't know where it will go. Probably, nowhere but here.

Alchemy of Shadow

A year ago, I rode my bike across town to buy a pregnancy test at the pharmacy. It was a hot day in early September and I pedaled home with one hand balancing the curled handlebars and the other clutching the paper bag that held a certain future. I had already sensed something shifting in me: a longing rose from my body, a new pulse and a need more powerful than the desire it usurped.

The plus sign began to form immediately—two blue lines criss-crossing. I set the plastic stick on the edge of the sink and walked away to wait the two minutes before I let myself believe. We lived then in an old house in Vermont. The bed stood beside a row of windows that bathed the room in the early autumn glow. The walls were painted baby blue and smooth river stones sat on the windowsills, along the lip of the bath, in the corners of rooms like spirits brought in from the cold. Sprawled on the oversized bed, I felt the scatter of light across my face as it weaved through the leaves of the ash trees in the yard—a twinkling of heat against my skin. A luminosity akin to water. I would study those trees for hours, nursing my grief—tall trees that had perhaps known generations of human life. But that day, as I waited for my husband's return, they radiated joy for the future I believed, without question, would be mine.

That summer I had discovered Andrea Modica's photographs of wild apple trees in the Northeast Kingdom of Vermont. Black-and-whites of feral trees in abandoned orchards blurred from focus, whirled up, spun out. In the eye of each storm, something offered, something given—a place for losing oneself, a union of shadow and land.

I worked on a farm at the time. Part of my job included driving a tractor that pulled a wagon of children and their keepers between the welcome center gift shop and children's farmyard. I coveted those two hours of sleepy driving, the mountains easing in and out of focus, the gift shop coffee always hot and fresh. I leafed through magazines and books of local poetry while I waited, sampling the farm's cheddar varieties meant for tourists and chatting up the clerk at the counter—farm gossip, weather, weekend plans. Century-old poplars lined the side of the trail I drove, the landscape unfolded into pastures speckled with sheep or the Brown Swiss dairy herd, and the mountains steeped in the colors of fall lay in the distance like sleeping wolves.

I discovered the photographs in the farm's gift shop, where I waited between tractor runs. *Pastoral* had done a story on the farm a few years ago and they sold the issue as a keepsake in the shop. Flipping through I found Andrea Modica's photographs near the end—the wild apple trees, the abandoned orchards, the Northeast Kingdom of Vermont.

Dark clots of fruit hung in slivered light; fallen apples lay like smudges, out of focus. The trees arrived out of the alchemy of shadow—a distance littered of light and darkness.

How I returned to those photographs all that fall. Standing amid the cheeses and T-shirts and goat's milk soaps, I combed the three or four pages of apple trees. I studied the mystery of shadow, the depth of light, and discovered in one woman's vision something revealed about the nature of our turning.

––––––––

The dream of them stayed with me a little as I drove down Poplar Drive, over the dirt and gravel, passing a field of Canadian geese gathered like tuxedoed men on their way south, then passing the grown spring calves close to slaughter. In everything a darkened mood that thrilled me.

Her photographs possessed the power to transform the afternoon, to pull me out of bouts of melancholy. In them I saw the world in terms of her visual distillations—a place of magic. The mystery of shadow, the depth of light unbound.

The sheep stood on the hill with their noses in the grass, their shadows dropped like stone spirits at their sides. There, a set of twin lambs, born out of season, still donned their long tails. Their white fleeces were a bold contrast against the ashen color of their mother's flank.

I kept a wary eye on the children as they scurried off the wagon and across the yard toward the animals in small pens. They dashed across the field as though the animals might be gone. And soon they would be. Every year new animals were born and slaughtered on the farm. The baby sheep that the children bottle-fed in the spring would be dead by November, killed as much for their inability to thrive without intervention or for their sex (we only kept the ewes) as for their meat. Then I drove the wagon back and returned to the photographs.

≈≈≈≈

Modica's lens ensnares the nature of loss and of longing. If nostalgia is the desire to return, to know again, to relive, *longing* carries the want for nostalgia over the thing that never was. *A longing more powerful than the desire it usurped.* The unrequited, the unknown grows ever larger in our hearts until it shipwrecks the body. We cannot breathe. We want and want again. The beloved. The alchemy of shadow—light and darkness filling form—roots here.

After I lost the pregnancy last year, I accused my husband of not wanting the child. "No," he answered me, "I felt only joy."

The artist gives us what we cannot give ourselves. No, that isn't it exactly. She offers this path—here, come, abandon—you will not return the same.

It was the beginning of October, weeks away from the end of the farm season. Josh drove me out of town and into the Vermont country, the trees ablaze with color. I closed my eyes. The sky felt too bright. Everywhere a nakedness interrupted. We had seen the heartbeat, that was all, and then it was gone. *What was that?* I grew sick as we drove.

"Please, take me back," I told my husband. "I can't stand this."

"I just wanted to see the leaves with you," he said, his voice desperate, small.

Home. I returned to the bed, the row of windows, the trees. To consider the patterns of light casting shadow into the sheets; to study the intricacies of branches, sky bound and ever expanding. How I might move my body so the light fell over my face, a scarf of warmth or an unbearable brightness. How the lightless corners of the room would grow, expand, and finally absorb me in consummate darkness.

And what is the nature of our turning? In the cycle of all things, a lost sense, a missing link.

Josh sliced tomatoes for sauce in the kitchen. Dozens of shiny reds from his father's garden sat in rows on the counter. I came in from smoking and stood beside him.

"You're smoking?" he said and began to cry.

We didn't understand what we had lost. I would insist to him that we had lost a child.

"It was not a child," he said.

"It would have been."

"Yes, but it wasn't."

Outside the leaves began to rustle free. Soon, we would begin timing ovulation, the hope for a child seeded in that first potential and its demise.

In one of Modica's photographs a single ruined apple, the size of a plum, dangles on a threadlike stem. The bare boughs ebb from focus into a timeless distance. The wrinkled fruit is captured in detail. The present hangs on, but not by much. Is the stem tough like fish wire or is it chance that held the fruit, soon to join the loamy earth below? The lens brings a singularity of focus to an arrested world. The white foreground of the photo misleads me into believing in just this one thing. Wanting, just this one thing. Holding on.

᪥᪥᪥᪥

All winter in Vermont we yearn for the land to return itself to us—a body frozen thaws—to birth and bring forth our second skin. But I wait instead for fall, always surprised by the longing that enters and empties me, that makes me believe in renewal all over again. The season catches me up in its dying color, its last blast of life, its firecracker brilliance; it cuts through me and reminds me that endings are beginnings and longing itself replaces what is lost for a while. There is pleasure in the perfection of such a well-made plan.

I find renewal in the turning of the season as in the turning of the body. But unlike the seasons, I can't be sure my body will turn again and so a distance grows of loss and envy.

It has been a year since we lost the first pregnancy. My belly grows with a new pregnancy as the weather turns—the beginning of another Vermont fall. One day while walking through the park across the street from our apartment, I think of Modica's photographs. I smell the cold smoky scent of autumn on the farm, feel the chill of the breeze pinking my cheeks, and remember the way my fingers grew cold, even in winter gloves, as I gripped the wheel of the tractor and drove out over the land.

I never thought to buy the journal with the photographs. Likely I wanted it to remain in the store, so I could return to it each day with a measure of surprise and longing.

We drove out on Route 7 and stopped at the farm's gift shop. It only took a minute for me to locate the journal with Modica's photographs. I flipped to the end almost surprised that they were still there. At first their beauty was lost on me. They were not as I remembered. Just as when we return to a childhood house—in memory, a palace—and see it through grown-up eyes. But then we are looking from a different place, looking with the intent of showing.

Perhaps the beauty exists for me alone. Only I know how to see the trees, the smudged apples, the sky and land bleeding into one another. Only I know how it feels.

I paid $9.50 for the journal and we left without seeing the farm—the sheep in the field, the Brown Swiss dairy herd, or the children's farmyard. It was closed for the season. We drove into the country, passing cornfields, old barns, and silos, not speaking, but watching, letting ourselves go a little in the last blaze of colors, the plum-hued mountains fading into the distance like smoke from an open fire.

And yet I want to show you.

☙ ☙ ☙ ☙

It had been on the farm when I began to bleed. Walking out to put the chickens in for the night, I felt the blood run warm between my legs. I stopped and called out to Elizabeth, something about using the restroom. She nodded, and I hurried through the farmyard to the lavatory, where I discovered bright red blood. *It's okay*, I told myself. *Nothing is wrong. Bleeding is normal.*

I called my husband and then went to wait for him in the parking lot. We drove home in silence, our hands wrapped safely together. When the clot passed, I felt its soft, warm presence slip loose. I touched a finger to the liver-colored thing in disbelief.

Long coil of breath rang from me, heaving shock in the golden light of the autumn afternoon.

I lay my cheek against the cold tile of the bathroom floor for a long time, before crawling into bed. My husband waited—helpless. Maybe he touched my cheek, held my hand, whispered love. I watched the trees in the light, meditating on each branch. My gaze followed limbs like braille for my eyes—I liked the thought of braille pressing into my eyes, softly imprinting words there: *leaf, sky, tree, lost.*

☙ ☙ ☙ ☙

I quit work at the farm five weeks before the season's official end. Months passed, and we moved from the blue room in the big old house with its looming trees to a tiny one-bedroom apartment beside a park. "Cozy," we said, and went on silently longing. Our wishes stretched between us, trellised with hope. Dark winter nights hung in the window, framing the quiet uncertainty of grief. Anger felt its way into the room where isolation muffled the rhythm of our solitary hearts pumping side-by-side all the long night. I missed the trees of the old house and wondered how they looked now, bare and shivering.

After Christmas I tacked pictures to the walls, organized bookshelves, and cooked lentil soup. The cold of January lulled me. We moved our bed into the living room, close to the apartment's only heater, and Josh spent weekends in it reading books and staring out the window at the glowing lawn of white in the park across the street.

I felt the sun reflecting against the awful white snow could burn something out of me. Afternoons, I walked out through the snow to the park across the street that overlooked Lake Champlain. The water froze to the breaker—a wall of stones that slowed the waves—past which it churned a blackened blue. I remembered my first year in Burlington. Walking on the shiny ice of the lake, the great expanse of frozen water stretched as far as I could see. I thought I could cross on foot and make it all the way to New York State. I wanted to unite with the winter beauty of this new city; yet, didn't a part of me also want to escape, to disappear into?

In every union something is abandoned.

And then it happened again: the blue lines crisscrossing in the turning light of February—hope sputtering forth, longing and relief. Fear. We sat on the bed in the living room and Josh said, "I don't want to get too excited."

"Can't you just believe?" I asked.

"I'll try."

"I know this time is different, please."

I never imagined I'd want a child in this way—the ache and pull of my body tethered me to this future love. Daydreams of my belly growing or the child in my arms interrupted my work hours, dropping me from the rhythm of daily life, only to leave me feeling the stab of longing edged with the fear of loss. Was it okay? Would the blood return? Was my body broken?

I thought of the farm at night in the dark lull before sleep. They would be lambing now. Waiting for life to come. Volunteers took night shifts, watching for a laboring ewe that might need the farmer's help. In the barn, a thin light colored the expectant ewes an unreal hue, and outside where the cold clouded one's breath, a million stars poured forth. In my bed at night with the street lights casting shadow over the room, I imagined those tiny lambs dropping from their mothers into the hay, entering the world during the coldest month of the year.

We were cautious about our joy. Silent. I kept a vigil, lighting candles and incense, and whispered prayers before the little altar I'd created. Two smooth stones, a beeswax candle, a bowl of birch bark from my childhood home, and sage. But it did not matter, I bled again and miscarried. Here, come, abandon—

⁂

I wanted to walk through Modica's orchards in the Kingdom, to blur into a body of shadow touching light. I wanted to pick the sour fruit of abandoned trees and bite into it. My mouth would quiver with shock. Light would echo into the haze of distance . . . grief weaving in and out, sewn into my fingers. Grief making patterns in my body, unseen, like shadows cast and swallowed by night.

What was there—a certain beauty—is here, come grief and secret sorrow. *In every union something is abandoned (not lost)*. "How far along were you?" friends asked, as if measuring my pain on a scale. It is true I did not hold a body. I did not mourn a stillbirth. It is true I might have asked the same question, unknowingly. But there is no language for miscarriage.

———————

There is a wild beauty in the excess and brevity of autumn—a second spring, they call the foliage bursting red, copper, gold. The empty boughs will stitch the gray skies of winter as the ephemeral nature of all things forges hope for something holy.

Hope also that something well loved might remain, and this we know shall not be true.

❧ ❧ ❧ ❧

All through February and into March I watched crows fly past our tiny apartment at dusk. A line of them scattered across the sky, flew south to roost in a nearby copse of trees. It often took a half hour for them to pass. I wanted to know where they were going and why they were here. But mostly I fell in love with the light at this hour, the light of winter's dusk. Regardless of the sounds in the midst, the light had a way of making silence and quieting the mind. The sky, turning shades of red and purple, strewn with clouds that skid into an immeasurable distance, morphed out a pattern of joining and releasing.

Grief follows no pattern—its shadow emerges from nowhere to nest in the belly, to birth from the mouth the sound of loss, hollowed into an echo, a repetition that incited rage in me. But the crows kept a schedule, followed a timetable, and returned to me the sky. Open, full, endless. They were shadows of the sky that seemed to whisper, *Here, come, abandon—*

I got the urge to follow the crows one afternoon and found hundreds roosting in a frozen tree near a cluster of trash bins in the parking lot behind the video store, China Buffet, and the post office. I went in and rented a movie.

❧ ❧ ❧ ❧

We have heard the heartbeat of this new baby, our third pregnancy, felt its quickening within, made a list of names (June, after my husband's grandma; Freya, for the Norse goddess; Moses, for the one who may call us to put forth our best selves; Felix, just because), and told our friends and family. Its life swells from my belly—a mystery of science and something holy. My body softens. I lay in the bath speaking to the child, with candlelight playing lambent over the little mound of growing babe. "You will love it here. I will teach you; I will show you how."

I imagine our child in my arms with his tender body wrapped against mine. How does one prepare for this? It feels impossible to comprehend that what is inside of me will soon be on the outside. For this short time, I am two and not one. How can an entire life exist within me? A life that will grow through the expanse of time, the distance of light and shadow; tethered of earth, a life that will turn as seasons and be gone.

We want, we want again—we grow mute with longing. In one woman's vision, I found grief over the misshapen world torn free. "Here," she said. "Come," she said. "Abandon." The alchemy of shadow roots here.

Ultima Thule

1. Ultima Thule: Of maps, the place beyond the known borders of the world.

2. There are those who don't believe in the outer rim of the known world, those who have not thought of it, and those, like me, who in longing, come to believe.

3. I walk along the shore in late October. My eyes trail the horizon across the lake, along the ridge of the mountains. Beneath the blue-gray sky, the last colors of fall emerge, a wash of orange-yellow-brown fading into the clay-mud hue of earth. Clouds no longer reflect in the choppy waters. Soon, black as stone, night falls.

4. Limit and limitlessness occur in all people, places, and things. But what are the boundaries of the body? How will we know to seek the uncharted realms of our being?

5. I have always been drawn to the white space of a page, where the underbelly of what language makes possible resides. I have always looked toward the sky for relief and sensed the outer rim of something not yet defined.

6. I move through the forest, my breath heavy with child. My heart pumps twice as much blood to keep my son safe in his burrow. Soon he will fatten and his feet, elbows, bottom will protrude from my belly. Soon he will begin his descent, his

passage from the netherworld—world beneath, world beyond. Gravity will take him, unravel his floating universe of complete warmth, and he will feel the weight of his body, of this living.

7. The trees with leaves burn orange to red, the floor of the forest softens underfoot from those already fallen. We pass an old farmstead and follow a stone wall made of the rocks settlers two centuries earlier cleared from the field. I am hot and then cold; my body is not my own.

8. The desire for dominion over the chaos of variables leads to all sorts of undoing—such as the cutting of babies from the womb and the lost art of birth.

9. When the time comes, fear overwhelms me. My son sits like a Buddha, stargazing in my womb. The doctors refuse to deliver a breech.

10. What tic in us, what bone or gene, what of the spirit longs for this beyond—great as territory or small as a babe—unbound by the mapped world, made of a language yet known? Genetic code or something holy, it calls to us. Come.

11. Ultima Thule: Of the mind, the limit of thought. Of the body, a landscape yet charted that shall come of touch, of space, of words, and not force, an intimacy with the unknown, with fear.

12. When they cut him from me he cries out only once. In pantomime, a single tear slips down my cheek. I feel its baptismal warmth pocket in my ear.

13. Love overwhelms. Bludgeons. Lays bare.

14. In the dream, my husband is many people at once asking me for my love. I follow him crying out: *Stop*. But always he shifts into someone new. In the dream, the trees of Socotra Island in Yemen climb the sky, their thick numerous branches grow up in a mushroom-cloud cluster.

15. I wrote a poem about the dream on the back of an old enve-
    lope, waiting for my love to return from the market, searching
    for the heart of something.

16. I wake from the dream and look at my husband, asleep in his
    beard of gold and brown. He is the same person—safe, easy to
    love.

17. Our lives are twined like grafted trees, cut and made new.
    Freedom grows of such commitment.

18. When we return home from the hospital, the mourning doves
    coo at my window. My hand on the baby's chest counts his
    heartbeat anew. No longer in the echo chambers of the womb.
    No longer side-by-side with my own.

19. There is nothing but the wet snow of February, the doves, and
    this child—

20. Will you seek the unknown, dear one? Will you wander—
    your holiness an offering?

The Highway Home

Northern Michigan opens like a gateway to my childhood. Near the Upper Peninsula, the forest along the highway turns from hardwood to coniferous, and I can feel the moisture receding from the air, the scent of pine seeping in through the open window. Late June, my husband, our baby son, and I cross the Mackinac Bridge with little fanfare on our way from Vermont to spend the summer with my family in northern Minnesota. In recent years, we stopped for pancakes in Mackinaw City, snapped photographs of the living statues painted gold or silver, waded into chilly Lake Michigan. In years to come, I imagine we'll do so again. But Moses, at four months old, isn't enjoying this ride, so as long as he's sleeping we'll keep to the road. Josh at the wheel, we head west on Highway 2 toward the boondocks of northern Wisconsin.

Highway 2 cuts through a landscape of beauty and desolation that composes the Upper Peninsula—craggy pine forests, pale sand beaches, and occasional wetland bogs with tree skeletons clustered like the naked masts of ships lost at sea. Small houses, some merely the size of sheds, with chipping paint and junkyard lawns appear along the highway. We pass few towns. Then a bar and a tiny gas station that regretfully only takes cash the elderly man explains from his perch behind a counter. He bats the air with his hand and tells me something about the price of those machines or bounced checks. But the people here are friendlier I think, unlike New Englanders who keep to themselves, mind their business at the grocery store. Though New Englanders fancy themselves look-you-in-the-eye friendly, it's nothing like the Midwest, where people talk to you like they've known you for years. I walk into a gas station and yawn. The middle-aged woman behind the counter calls out to me, "Don't be doing that in here, it's contagious." She smiles at me. I think of my own mother's gentle sarcasm and the gratuitous friendliness known as "Minnesota nice."

Occasionally I spot a manicured lawn, a fenced garden, a potted geranium hanging from a porch awning, or a window box of marigolds, and this dedication to beauty and order pleases me. I am drawn to these unassuming homes, and the monotony of the road leads me to imagine the lives of the people who inhabit them. The solace of reverie is the only cure for boredom on the road. It is only now, having lived away from rural life for years, that this landscape strikes me as both foreign yet subtly familiar. For the landscape in which I came of age, that molded me and fed my imagination, that held me in its wildness until I spoke the language of trees, lakes, dirt, and sky, no longer feels like home—like breath and body—though I call it that. Where this passage begins—the gates of the Mackinac, the shores of Lake Superior, or the country roads unraveling through forest—so too the grand theater of memory and imagination follows, one becoming the other becoming the other in a perpetual Möbius strip of who we are, were, and hope to be. We are never the same and each moment gives way to a new remembering of what has been. Does memory filter the present or the present filter memory? Which version of the story will carry us into tomorrow, and once we choose it, will we ever be able to return and choose differently?

From my passenger seat, I see a woman crouched in her garden, hatless in the sun. I consider who she is, was, and hopes to be. What is she growing, where do her children live if she has them? Does she mind the sound of traffic or has it long ago receded from her notice? We pass an old boarded up summer home, half-finished, it's windows still covered with stickers announcing their maker. I imagine a family running out of money in the middle of construction and moving away. Somewhere a woman stands in her suburban kitchen, eyes out the window on the overfertilized lawn, and she recalls this view of the great blue lake—endless and wild. If she closes her eyes she can smell the pine forest, hear the soft waves of Lake Michigan, feel the give of the boat beneath her body as she motors out from shore. For a moment, she touches that wildness that soothes something in her, its flame ignites and she has not abandoned herself, no, she realizes, despite the drudgery of daily life, she can still find her way back, she still hungers.

I ask my husband what he thinks about the people of Highway 2 in northern Wisconsin. "This highway is odd, don't you think?" I say, trying to sound casual, to not reveal that I've already created a narrative of these people's lives, already imagined the details of their homes and hearts. "Where do you suppose these people work? What do you think they do?" He keeps his eyes on the road. His Red Sox cap is pulled down over a mess of greasy road hair.

"Hard tellin' not knowin'," he says in his best Vermont redneck accent. He is an overeducated mountain boy himself. I grunt; he smirks.

"Fascinating insight," I say.

"Yep."

"I know you don't *know*. I'm asking what you *think*. You know, what kind of assumptions do you make about the people of this highway—what is it like here?"

"Like I said, hard tellin' not knowin'," and I know without looking there's a gleam in his eye as he says it.

Josh and I share certain traits, but he's intuitive while I'm imaginative. He believes in ghosts and animal spirits, recounts his nighttime dreams to his kindergarten students during morning meeting and asks them to share their own. He declares allegiance to all sorts of mystical experiences, including one where he floated up to the ceiling. Yet he prefers not to imagine the intricacies of the lives of others in the wildly subjective ways I'm fond of. So, while I would like to share my fantasies with him, the people of the highway will remain my secret. "Aren't you at all interested?" I urge, one last time.

"No."

I glimpse an old man on his riding lawn mower, cutting a square patch of lawn around his small house, his forehead polished with sweat in the afternoon sun. Who is he? What does he love?

We pass a small lake with rippling waters, tiny waves gallop. We pass Ashland, Wisconsin, where a few years ago I attended a concert with my mother, aunt, and cousins, and where two years ago, on our drive, I bought orange cheese late at night, desperate for something more substantial than gas station food. Last year, pregnant, I procured organic fruit for a small fortune at the co-op in the college town of Marquette, Michigan. These landmarks comfort me, as though moving through a loved one's home, touching objects that you've come to recognize over the years. They make the drive feel less daunting, and now on our third year of repeating this journey, these landmarks also forebode an emotional unrest lingering in me. Home is a refuge sometimes encumbered by sorrows from my former life. I get stuck in the webbing of the old grief. I stayed away for years, unable to return for more than a week or so, unwilling to face who I was, who I had been, or what still lay unwelcome, beneath the surface. But my love for my four sisters, my brother, my mother and father always leads me back.

What is it we remember, anyway? Everything of the past makes itself known only through the singularity of any moment in which we find ourselves, and what we have been thinking of, longing for, hurting over always shines the view. Who hasn't yearned for a relationship to be another way, wanted so much to be well loved? Yet perhaps in so doing we foreclose the possibility of what might be, might have been. We lose. And what can we know of those we've lost, who have passed from living into the wide breath beyond, who have passed from fluid existence into the haze of our remembrance, who in longing go back into the waves, go diving into the wreck?

The world, after all, is in us, not us in the world, or so they say. When I began writing these essays, home meant something different than it does today. What I know about the world, how I feel my way through it, can only be my story—as flawed and broken as that truth is, it is still the only one I have.

We pass an ornate house with dozens of windows framed in white, reflecting the blue of the sky. It would be out of place, but the junk pile yard reminds me that dreams are hard to keep up. I go back to imagining the people of the highway, Josh still at the wheel. I see shelves of porcelain figurines, spoon and thimble collections, old La-Z-Boys with doilies on the arm cushions and grease stains where heads rested for too long. I smell kitchens with meat cooking, noodles boil and steam the windows, plates laid out on Formica tabletops with paper napkins in their plastic holders. I imagine lean men in work shirts and jeans, with thin hair parted on the side like my Grandpa Ray's, my mother's father, walking slowly down the road, heads bowed after a full day's work, to the bar where they will stand out back and smoke their cigarettes, coughing and hacking up phlegm and spitting it out in quick, successive swills. Looking out at a copse of birch, oddly out of place in the sea of pines, one man remembers something from boyhood: a slurred image, the sound of a river, a flash of red from a ten-speed, the smell of his mother's lap where he pushed his face, rubbed his snotty nose as a young boy; who he once was and hoped to be.

He remembers this in the same way that he glances at the familiar faces in the bar, nodding hello, both knowing and not knowing them. In the same way that the sound of a train sends a shimmer through his groin, makes him long for elsewhere without him even realizing it anymore. He stubs out his cigarette and his brain mechanically shifts to a list of bills, chores, his wife's grievances, as he enters the dimly lit bar, TVs ablaze on the wall. He drinks beer until his body feels the numb relief he has craved every day of his life since the first day he drank beer until his body felt numb with relief. He wants for another time, nostalgia covers him like grief, the grief that comes from wanting, from insatiable longing, and the imagined past.

I am thinking about my grandfather, a man who in the last years of his life sat in a La-Z-Boy drinking cans of beer at night, smoking cigarettes, and watching TV until he passed into sleep. Though I remember little about him, every memory is good and kind. We shared the disease of alcoholism and some days I want to ask what happened to him, how he became a gentle drunk, one who, according to my mother, on certain days in certain years merely drank himself to sleep at night. Though I doubt this was the only damage, I know that he managed to live a functional life until his early death of cancer at sixty-four. I also know that he never considered himself a drunk and so there is little he could have told me and yet I hold him like a myth in my mind, the secret broken soul in my line of genetics, the key to something. But what?

In the history of my life, his death when I was eleven marked a turning point in my family, like stumbling from the Garden of Eden. He died during my golden years just before puberty, when we girls tend to be fully ourselves, unaware of the cruel expectations that would soon be forced on us. His death became a bend in my river, a turn toward rapids that built like a fugue as I became more and more aware of the intricacies of my mother's family. Years later I would read my aunt's poetry: "That summer I read the Russians and drank too much wine." And I would understand exactly what she meant because I too spent many summers in similar fashion, chasing the end of a bottle and the great literature of the world until I could no longer stop drinking too much wine, and my life, I saw, had fallen apart. But the Russians, they are still my good friends.

Memories collect and the more I recall and recount them the smoother they grow like stones in the river of my mind. They become bountiful ruins that I return to, I cultivate and nurture as my own mythology. If home is anything, it is myth and magic and at the very least the start of the story. Home pulls me back like an axis of life, a place I return to both to tear myself open and to find healing renewal in a landscape that soothes me with a language unlike others.

Lured by the yellow sands and cool-blue waters of Lake Michigan, Josh and I stop at a beach. I carry the baby down to the shore and lay him on the blanket, careful to keep his delicate skin covered. Josh braves the frigid waters, not yet warmed from the months of summer. I half want to follow him in but the idea of finding my swimsuit, or rather the postpregnancy yoga gear I'm using for a swimsuit, deters me. For a few minutes, we try to battle the unexpected sandflies, hoping the wind will pick up. But they get the better of me and I insist on returning to the car and the air-conditioning to nurse Moses. He plays on a pillow on my lap for a while, happily sucking his fingers, free from the restraints of his car seat.

Then it's back to the highway with the sun burning down, the sky a wash of blue, the craggy jack pines or red and white pines growing like giants beside the road, and the feel of sand in our toes. I fall asleep and wake as we cross the Superior bridge into Minnesota and the city of Duluth. I once spent a semester of college here, listening to the foghorns call from the lake and studying the poets of modernity. Passing the shipyards, I look up at the hill lit against the night with the glow from houses and streetlamps. From here, we drive two hours north and reach my parents' log home in the woods of northern Minnesota, traveling finally down a dirt driveway filled with potholes to our destination.

As I carry the sleeping baby up the path, I'm no longer worried about the other selves or the other lives. I am full with the pathos of the night sky, imbued with the contours of the universe—a blizzard of stars and the blur of the Milky Way. The spikey heads of pines point to the netherworld above. We leave unpacking for the morning, and after my mother and father peek at Moses, I nestle him between pillows in the bed of the guest room, once the childhood bedroom I shared with my sister Hannah. When my head hits the pillow, I think of the people of the highway: the man on his riding lawn mower, the one I imagined in the bar, and the woman in her kitchen. They belong to a faraway land, but like all citizens along the road to my childhood kingdom, I carry their whispered missives with me, a secret power, a well-worn prayer.

Reverence Song

Summer. The boy down the street drowned. Ten years old, their only child. This is not my sorrow to have and to hold; still, when I walk past their house with my son, I look for them—the man and his wife. I know I shouldn't, but how can I not? I consider the flowers along the walkway to their small gray house on my afternoon jog—daylilies, sweet william, and foxglove. A row of hollyhocks near the fence. All perennials. One night, alone, I peer in the window and see a child's drawing of a cheetah framed and hanging on the wall. I remember that the boy was an artist. Last year everything bloomed, then summer rose, like an overgrown yard turned to meadow, and flourished. My husband said: "I've seen the father and he's a shell of a man." I turned the phrase in my mind, *a shell of a man*, what did it mean? I wanted then to touch their bodies, to feel their clammy skin in my hands, to palm their faces and kiss their thorny mouths. I wanted to know what it was to survive. My son was four months old.

A former lover once sent me a poem by Galway Kinnell; the poet writes about the birth of a child:

> they hang her up
> by the feet, she sucks
> air, screams
> her first song—and turns rose,
> the slow,
> beating, featherless arms
> already clutching at the emptiness.

I had no children at the time, but the poem stayed with me, a rosary in my mind—both warding off and calling forth the paradox of giving life, giving death.

Summer. I stand on the sidewalk at dusk and watch wild geese fly north—crying, crying into dark night. The American flag, strung up on a poll, snaps in the wind, a sharp, familiar noise. When I look back, the V is gone, the night quiet. Ahead of me my husband pushes our one-year-old son in the stroller. I have lagged behind, tired, restless. Rain brought the end of a humid spell. The day was blue skied, cool with lofty clouds. In the afternoon, I scooped up my red-haired boy and whispered in his ear, *you* are all I've ever wanted. It startled me to say that. I pressed my lips to the soft pillow of his cheek. He threw back his head and laughed, then brought his small hands to my face and pressed them into my cheeks. His blue eyes mirroring mine.

Summer. We used to covet night. My not-yet-husband and I. Sitting at outdoor café tables in town, sipping whiskey on ice or cold pints of beer, listening to country bands or acoustic guitars strummed by young men in love. We got drunk and he drove us to the beach, it was the only place I wanted. Not home, no, never home. I didn't want the night to end. Swimming, the moon hung amid the bramble of clouds. Its dappled light fell where the water shoaled, and we plunged in and floated face up, bodies freed. Sometimes a lone sailboat drifted at the edge of our swimming cove, and I thought of all the places I wanted to go, and other times we lost each other in the shadow of trees or the darkness of a new moon night but never for long. In the sunlight, our love felt fragile, but not there in the dark, our bodies wet and kissing.

Summer. The loon calls deep into the night. As a child, I slept all summer in the loft of a cabin beside a murky lake. Some nights I climbed into bed between my parents. Their bed lay level with the open window, and on my belly, I could look out into the night and the lake, could seek the moon in its bed of sky. There in the cold of the lake the loons cried, a fluted howl, an echo that reverberated in my chest, stuck in my own throat, paddled at the rivers of my heart. The call of the loon still haunts me when I hear it, visiting my parents in Minnesota, my son asleep beside me. It's a beautiful haunting, a way of aching. And like muscle memory, I slip into the intimacy of longing.

Summer. Late August, the boy and his friend were swimming in a river. Wading in up to their boney knees, skipping rocks where the water lay smooth. When the current took the boy under with unforeseen strength, his friend caught his hand. They held onto each other as long as they could but the waters pulsed fierce, a force no child could match. I imagine their two hands wound together in the gush of the river water, cold and blue. Commotion on shore in the wake of the slow realization, then panic. A father trying to reach the boys, a mother running. There's a breeze in the trees along shore, and a lone cloud sunk in acres of sky. The cry comes almost before their hands release. Then the boy is gone and there is only one hand, *already clutching at the emptiness.*

Summer. If I learned only one song it would be this song.

Prayer for the
Scavenger World

I think of her when I pass the pickers along the road, catching only a glimpse of bodies crouched low in the brush. They hover above blueberry bushes, their fingers turning plum as they pick, their mouths wet with glee. Years ago, our mothers tied bandanas around our heads, sprayed us with DEET to keep the bugs away, and took us berry picking. All summer we lived among the trees in wooden cabins with paths to the lake, the sauna, the outhouse, the neighbors, and our fort. This place—childhood—carved a hole the shape of God in our chests.

I turn and head into the forest where I jog past rows of Norway pine on a soft path. My breath comes fast; sweat beads at my temples. The symmetry of the trees reminds me of warriors waiting, ready. But too, they could be saintlike statuary caught reaching for the sky, frozen but for the wind.

I want to forgive her for going back to the addict's life. I want to bind my cruelty, tether my rage, drown my sense of righteousness. Sometimes, though, I just want to hate her for leaving me to navigate this sober path alone. I sense in these trees, here, now, that I won't see her again for a long time and when I do she won't be the same. Nothing ever is.

The pickers know when to go. They have their secret spots. Some cultivate private berry patches in backyards or fields, along chain-link fences and highways. They grow raspberries as big as thimbles, blueberries like marbles. But most go in secret to the wild, covetous of what the earth gives freely. They return filled with the joy of the scavenger, the pleasure of the hunt, already planning their next excursion. Every year, come July, I start to see evidence of them along the road—an old Ford pickup waiting, the gray van covered in rust, a pair of bicycles lying side-by-side like lovers tangled in embrace.

I admire their persistence—whole days in the berry patch, buckets procured for winter's bounty or canned jam—and yet I am not one of them. I want to tangle my bike with another's or buy a straw hat for picking. I want to brag of secret fields where I discovered untouched bushes as far as I could see, burn my arms in the sun for the glory of nature's jewels. Instead I run through the forest heaving until my lungs grow fierce, near the end of summer. I will promise myself not to give up running come winter, though I always do.

Grandma hated picking, though she came along to bitch and moan about the heat and the flies—and how we loved her for it! Our mothers took us kids: seven little girls crammed into the back seat of the long-assed Plymouth her mama drove years past the paid off date, a point of pride. All things that lasted pleased our mothers as though they'd hit a lottery of luck in an old car still running, a kitchen stove that worked long past its prime, or leather sandals worn for a decade. Like blond bandits, the two sisters traveled dirt roads in search of the best picking, singing songs out of tune, laughing until they cried. Their children, yet unmarred by this life, sang along.

I am learning to lose her again, dear girl, my surrogate sister, to this disease. The same one that took our grandfather and derailed the lives of her mother and our uncle nearly destroyed my own.

No one ever told us the truth, or perhaps no one ever knew the truth—we would stop at nothing to "take the edge off" of life. Our longing grew into a singular point, the pinprick of a star, into one thing alone. We were ravenous for escape—no longer wild and free but birds caught in a trap that made us crazed. How that bitter song has touched each one of us in one way or another—my sisters and hers, the seven of us. Our mothers. Our fathers. Still we longed to catch that first sweet high again, to chase that nascent relief we knew like a first love until we were dead in the trap.

Somehow, I got free. But she didn't. Hasn't. Yet. Will again? Sometimes I still hear her voice, like vespers from the other side, calling me back. But mostly I've given up on her and it feels like a turning away from the night sky. Silence, like an open wound and an emptying of blue. What choice do I have? I'll never save her.

I want to nurse my anger, not to crouch in silence, patient, hopeful, speaking prayers as I fill my bucket. *Don't take her. Protect her. Please, God.* God of the summer sky, God of strong water, God of paths that lead to bonfires, God of the quiet earth where the berries grow and little girls pluck them to place like candy on the bed of their small tongues. Where little girls make stories of the trees and swing out over the lake on a rope and let go. Slip into the slick embrace of water, deep as sky.

I run harder, longer, further, faster. Someday I think I'll shake this sorrow, shake the genes right out of me so they never touch my own children. Somehow, I think, I'll inoculate them from this obsession, one their father's family has known just as intimately as mine.

Why am I angry? Why turn my back on her now? It's been years. I'm tired of living clenched with fear—not knowing. Tired of imagining her blue body and what I will say to her when she's dead. Everything I can't say now because she's too far away even when she's beside me. I have no right to my anger. Still I let it brim up. Let it spill.

Through the forest, passing rows of warrior trees, passing the gentle God of wind and a clan of women crows caught up in flight, I run. I am not a runner, but I run. Each breath, each footfall, a humble prayer caught up in the lungs of the world.

One year, as girls, perhaps the last year we went berry picking with our moms and sisters and Grandma, we teased our home-permed hair and covered it with hair spray; she loaned me a tie-dyed smiley face shirt in neon colors. At the patch, we feigned exhaustion and lay together on the ground moaning. Our mothers laughed at their preteen daughters who might have been twins. Somewhere there's a picture of us sprawled in that berry patch, our arms around each other, our sticky hair spiked high above our flushed cheeks. Somewhere, those girls live on.

Come August this year the pickers are gone.

The sky at night as I walk through the forest, sleepless and worried, reminds me of insurmountable distances—lifetimes cast asunder, childhood, the richness of a gentle God. Forgiveness.

Every life carries with it a universe of arms reaching out to gather back a million force fields, and when it's gone it takes with it all the stars that cast light, leaving layers of darkness into which the living fall. She is not dead, but still I feel her absence. I slip into the shadows where once she lived, where we once walked together down a path through the woods in a kingdom the shape of God, the place we will always long for. But perhaps longing becomes a pleasure all its own, and we are merely an amalgamation of all our selves—all the girls we once were and the lands beloved.

———

I look for the constellation of Pleiades, the seven sisters, rising over the tree line in the forest as I walk, but I can never find it. I smile and remember how we huddled together as girls in the berry patch, our hair coated with hairspray, our neon bobby socks, our smiley face T-shirts—"Don't Worry Be Happy"—dear girl, our hearts seeded together in this scavenger world.

Body of Memory,
Phoenix of Time

I.

Last night at the Massachusetts Museum of Contemporary Art in North Adams, we dined at banquet tables beside the Chinese artist Xu Bing's *Phoenix* birds. Lit up and hanging, the birds are the size of small sailboats and made completely of scraps salvaged from construction sites in urban China. My son, Moses, ran beneath the birds, tossing his toy horses and yelling "giddyap." He broke a plate with glee and the staff appeared like secret police to clear away the wreckage—white porcelain sails, sharp as knives. We returned to our wedding supper of eggs and waffles and breakfast sausage. Moses stuffing his mouth with blueberries, my husband drunk on champagne and orange juice, our dear friend married.

Then home. Just past dusk, I lie in bed beside Moses. Halfawake, I sing as I nurse him to sleep. Thunder rings and lightning flashes, a late summer rainstorm. The outline of the tree in the yard pulses in my window and reminds me of the imprint of memory—the flare of recollection. I think of the awful pain of time and the way (I once heard a poet on the radio say) myth connects us to eternity.

I am reminded of the part of me that would prefer a life as a hermit in the woods, though with a family, with children. How much I love children and never knew until I had my own and my sisters had theirs and they clung to my side with their sticky hands and hot breath and whispers. Their voices so tender, I might cry over them.

Place forms its own kind of time and its own myth. I live between two landscapes: the woods of northern Minnesota and Burlington, Vermont. It is early September and just before the wedding we had returned from spending the summer at my family's home in Minnesota. We left the pine forests, the shallow lake, and the sky like a wild creature. We left the dirt roads of my childhood, the trails into the woods leading to berry patches and rows of planted pines, where I ran in quiet reverence. We returned to our home in Vermont: a city beside a long, deep lake that carries sailboats all summer, boats that I watch with longing but have never sailed.

2.

At night in Minnesota, in the dark between the lake and the sauna, I lay on the dock under the stars, the silence cut only by the cry of loons. The sky here is bigger, I think, and I remember that this is something a friend wrote to me in a letter one summer between college semesters. It is an image I have coveted my whole life. The sky here feels closer without the reference point of mountains or tall buildings.

Days before I left, I stood with Moses in the heat of an open field. I watched my mother, crouched in the brush, picking blueberries. All I could see of her was a broad-rim straw hat and her thin, tanned shoulders. I sat down and gave Moses what berries I had picked to eat, not more than a few cups. I have never been patient enough to berry pick for long; my restless mind dreams of elsewhere, wanders through lists of tasks, books, projects I habitually plan. But I want to be that kind of person, the kind that can lose herself to hours of berry picking, devote herself in meditation to the act of creating sustenance. It was a good year for blueberries and the annual pickers had been out in droves. I saw the same pickup trucks and rusty minivan parked along the road for days when I jogged.

My sister Bess came from the field with a full container. She stood with her palms brushing the sides of her legs, her long hair tied back under her own straw hat. If I saw her from a distance walking on the road, she looked identical to my mother—something about their hips, thin legs, and rounded shoulders, the sway of body. She seemed suddenly shy before she told me that she was pregnant. "Oh, good," I may have said, reaching out to hug her. The sky that afternoon was blue and flanked with clouds, the wind, only a murmur. In six months, she would birth a red-haired girl and name her Alma.

I can still smell the scent of woodsmoke from the sauna fire and from the bonfire where I sat that last night in Minnesota with my brother and Bess. We did not speak but looked into the flames knowing already how to leave each other with little fanfare. The other end of leaving was harder for me. I cried for three days when I returned to Vermont, worried that I was living the wrong life. That I too should remain in the rural north woods of Minnesota, wandering the forest trails, paddling a kayak on a quiet lake, and cross-country skiing across the snow-covered frozen waters of winter. But I could not stay there. I needed people who were different than those I'd grown up with. I needed other landscapes. I needed the distance that myth is made of and a sky fortressed by mountains.

At the fire that night, I marveled over the shapes of poppy-orange coals. Sensing in the dark that our bodies were moving through time faster and faster, spinning out and collecting new worlds in our separate paths—how long could we remain tied to the familiar bonds of this home? The home where first love grew beside first sorrow, first longing, first humiliation and comfort. Would we hold on and remain faithful to this first landscape? Or would we, when our parents died, fight over the land, someone insisting on a sale, rendering the land orphaned, it's particular language, the landscape as we spoke of it and as we made it, lost. What would happen to the parts of me that are made of that land and that only in those woods, beside that lake, found communion?

In the dark of the thunderstorm the memory of the fire and the field recede, sure to resurface and thread through my days. What has been lingers and takes shape as it drifts through the moment of the present. We remember, we reshape, we tell again, if only to ourselves, this story—whatever it is—and it imbues the fabric of a new landscape.

3.

I can still feel the grass in my hands as I braid it and fasten it to a stick that I hang between two birch trees to make a curtain for my fort at ten years old. I can smell the ice of the pond and hear the scrape of my skate blade, feel the place on my scarf that has grown wet from breath and begun to freeze, more than twenty years ago now. Not last week or yesterday afternoon—I remember nothing of them—but years ago, decades now. To blow hot breath where my scarf has frozen stiff, I remember, just as I remember the way the pine trees stood dressed in snow circling the pond, and the angle of the sun on a winter's afternoon, hugging the southern horizon, dropping away before the afternoon had a chance to take shape. And why do I covet these memories? Recasting them here on the page, reshaping them in my mind, collecting them like a menagerie of little beasts, of which I am keeper and custodian. What is this longing for the little girl that built doll houses from scraps of wood and glue, pounding nails into tiny beds made from the end of boards her father used to build their family home? I suppose we are all caught in this swan song in one way or another. The grief of time passed.

In her essay "A Sketch of the Past," Virginia Woolf writes, "Those moments—in the nursery, on the road to the beach—can still be more real than the present moment." She recalls in tender detail the sound of the waves from her nursery window where she laid, "the waves breaking, one, two, one, two, and sending a splash of water over the beach" and the scuttle of the little bead on the end of the curtain blind as the wind blew it across the nursery floor. As children we are taken up fully by experience. We remember the details of the world with the vivid memory of the body. We record in color, in sound, in smell, in touch. Woolf believed that as we age we develop explanations for our experiences. We categorize and stereotype experience as we see through the lens of all the sensory data we've collected. Perhaps we process memory differently. With age, then, "this explanation blunts the sledge-hammer force of the blow" of experience and memory.

Woolf names the rare moments when the truth of our existence flickers through "moments of being." *The scuttle of the little bead as the wind blew it across the nursery floor.* "These moments of being of mine were the scaffolding in the background; were the invisible and silent part of my life as a child," Woolf writes. Moments of being are sparks: a flickering we cannot catch but that catches us and holds us to the light of what it means to be human, to live in time and space among others, to love and grieve and know that it will end.

4.

Xu Bing's *Phoenix*, one male, one female, came alive with a certain irony as we supped on lavish breakfast foods in the hanger-sized room of the Mass MoCA, in love with love. Robed in exquisite garments to attend the decadent banquet of matrimony, we too are not what we at first appear to be. And why is it that nearly everything I thought was true, all the lavish understandings of language, the words and gods of my youth, unravel under the lens of time? Only ambiguity, curiosity, and wonder, only beauty and its seeking, only the offering of a love imperfect, has kept.

Feng and *Huang*, majestic creatures made of trash in perpetual flight, are not what they appear to be and yet they are. At first sight they are beauty. Closer, we see their odd material. They are composed of the remnants of human toil, of suffering, and corruption. Xu began his project in his homeland just before the 2008 Olympics when the government's gentrification project was underway in Beijing. Historically, most governments displace their citizens in order to build their Olympic playgrounds. Unsightly housing is destroyed, leaving the occupants homeless. A Chinese real estate developer originally commissioned the project. The birds were meant to hang in a glass atrium connecting the two towers of the Chinese World Financial Center. But when Xu saw the construction sites for the towers he was stunned by the working and living conditions of the migrant workers and he proposed using debris from these sites for the birds.

The phoenixes are made of demolition debris: steel beams, rebar, shovels, gloves, hoses, hard hats, jackhammers, remnants of the daily lives of migrant laborers. Before he lost the commission for the birds, he was asked to coat them in crystal—cover over all that detritus. He refused, knowing it would destroy the integrity of his work. Parceled-together scraps—junk really—the birds were transformative. They told the story of the plight of the Chinese people who with the onslaught of globalization have been forced into industrial slavery. Xu made the phoenixes rise from the garbage, a signal of hope, a reversal of their traditional meaning in Chinese culture—royalty and dynasty—a new myth for his people.

5.

Some days I remember the depth of my inner life before I had a child, a husband, an incessant need to clean, keep house, make money, and I feel besieged by grief. Once I lived in collusion with the poets. Once I lived alone. Their words spoke to me in my bones, my organs, my skin, the ends of my fingers, my hair—in the place that we go when we stand at the window with the lightning so near and the thunder booming—Woolf's moments of being. Words were close to my body, sewn into my skin, but what did I know then, at twenty or even twenty-nine?

Eliot's *Four Quartets* haunted me for years. Coming back like a drum rhythm, "What might have been and what has been /

Point to one end, which is always present." But do I still believe that? Was Eliot trying to sweeten his mistakes with poesy? Am I? I want to believe his one end is more than a fancy way to speak of death. I want to believe that all time unwinds into one home, and the body too a place of comfort, to refuse a linear existence. Instead I face the grief of memory. The angst of knowing what has been will never come to pass again. I long for the immediacy of the world that I felt as a child and that only through poetry, nature, or the magic of art have I again glimpsed. But that such glimpses exist should be enough for gratitude.

Perhaps it was my life with the poets—the lover of words—that steeled me for the life of now, a scaffolding of rhyme and image, of subversive allegiance to the myth of the phoenix, the story of rising again and of return, despite everything. It is my son and husband who tether me to this world. Pulled abruptly into the moment of the present by the constant needs of a small child, the past ducks back into its rightful corner. I am full with the landscape of this present, where time runs like a water through my fingers and the floors are forever dirty and there is never enough money, but I am mostly content.

6.

We forget the slowness of the child's world. Wherein the body swims free, the world loosens. We cherish the child and the childlike perspective. Yet we do not want to be children, we don't even really want to act like them. What we want is to return. Nostalgia means longing for home—the home of memory, lodged in the construct of time. But to what shall we return? To the timelessness of youth? To this unbroken first act that we have replayed in the mind year after year until what remains is a memory as smooth as a worry stone in the rough palm of time.

"Life is first boredom, then fear," the poet Philip Larkin wrote. Fear is always fear of our own end. *A sky fortressed by mountains. The scuttle of the little bead. She listens for a different way of know-*

ing. Point to one end. "Whether or not we use it," Larkin writes, "it goes."

Story becomes our attempt at stopping time by containing it and myth the thrust of language toward eternity, a stifling of our own end. Yet I sit in meditation attempting to touch eternity, to quell the words of thought, the awe-full language of being. I sit breathing away the story.

There is something in our brokenness—fragmented time—which we long for. We know that experience is fragmented: time bends in on itself, time escapes us, and time evades what is real about the experience of our humanness. Fragmentation gets at the real.

Distance creates longing and what is time if not distance, the distance between my body then and my body now, between when we were together and when we were not. Still, time touches the human body and civilization and nothing else. All else is cyclical, regenerative. Time is a function of language and we are a construct of language. Time is our ruler and memory our rebellion. Hear the waves from the nursery, as she listens for a different way of knowing.

7.

Xu Bing's work takes up the notion of false appearances and the question of how language communicates: How do we make meaning, and how do we tell our stories and fashion our myths? Xu's *A Book from the Sky* first appeared in 1988 at the National Museum of Fine Arts in Beijing. For this work, he invented four thousand characters that resembled Chinese and printed scrolls of text with them. The exhibit featured four hundred handmade books using traditional Chinese typesetting, binding, and stringing techniques laid out in a grid over the floor. Fifty-foot-long printed scrolls hammocked the ceiling; there were wall panels printed in the style of Chinese newspapers. Inspired by traditional Chinese printing, which uses hand-carved woodblocks for each character, the work took Xu three years to create.

Some Chinese viewers expected to read the texts. Confused by the invented characters, some viewers sought to locate meaning or identify pattern in the work, but there was none. Reactions to the exhibit varied and some expressed anger toward Xu's art. Later, on display in the West, those who could not read Chinese did not suspect the falsity of the characters—the work took on new meaning. Perhaps, in the West, the work brought together viewers through a shared experience of language rendered unintelligible, a childlike understanding of text, a comingling of cultures.

A Book from the Sky was immediately lauded as a major work in China. But after Tiananmen Square, the following year, during which government-ordered military intervention led to the massacre of hundreds of protesters, the communist government criticized Xu for his work. He was placed under surveillance and shortly thereafter immigrated to the United States. He would later return to Beijing in 2008 as an internationally admired artist. At the time, Xu was quoted saying, "The reason people had so many reactions to *A Book in the Sky* is because it didn't say anything." Language rendered meaningless is a crime against the government.

8.

Memory fills me with a longing for home. Don't we always long for home? Home: a landscape like the body, shifting and filling as time shuffles on. The body homes us in memory—the other lives and selves we've lived and been. Like the phoenix rising we may erect this past to our liking—beauty lit up and hanging in defiance of the king ruler, time. Let us create our own myths and imbue them with their own power. Let us listen for the many ways of knowing. Let us lie down in the sand of the beach with the nursery song of waves at our feet and think of nothing but sky.

Now I am standing in my body, with its paper-thin lines thickening with every new moon, holding my own child in my arms, sensing already how soon he will grow into eight years old, into that awkward twelve, how he will swan into twenty, and be gone.

Here I am again, sitting at my little desk writing these thoughts. Here I am nursing the baby who is no longer a baby but a toddler. Here I am again trying to eat the fall apples in Vermont, but my teeth are too sensitive so instead I find myself standing in the supermarket, running my fingers over the russet apples, skins like the finest of sandpaper. And yes, I slip through again, hear the scuttle, and now I am nine, sanding wood for the dollhouses I made with my father's wood scraps and I can smell the wood glue and feel the presence of my mother's body, a kind of bliss.

The storm quiets and Moses sleeps and I kiss his cheek and my husband's cheek and go into the kitchen and eat some ice cream. In the calm and silence, I feel my entire life unspooling like thread. Not from here to there, but a messy pool of string, knotted and tangled. The present interwoven through the past, and though I cannot define it, I sense the future rests too in my body. I listen to the silence and think of all the other silences, and all the other landscapes that weave in and out through my mind at any given moment, in time, because what other way is there to know, to understand than this? But the *Phoenix*, my God, lit up and hanging, it was brilliant to see.

Beneath a Sky of Gunmetal Gray

But doesn't the universe also fix on falling sparrows, lend
its attention to spectacular disaster, train its very steady
eye on accidents, suffering, diminishment?

—LIA PURPURA

Bird

In her hands, a small bird like an organ stitched outside the body,
delicate and feathered. The bird has died and she carries the car-
cass, which to her is still the bird. Its liquid-black eyes are pupil-
less and from its mouth a drop of blood spills. It had flown into the
window.

Rabbit

My brother is a boy and there is my sister, also a child, with her
white-blond hair, the day she killed a rabbit. It was an accident.
She dropped the tiny creature. It curled its spine as it fell, stretched
its body as though reaching for her. I could see what was about to
happen. The neck of the rabbit snapped at the spine upon landing.
She bent and cupped the limp rabbit in her hands.

"Oh," I said, "it's okay." I wanted to comfort her. "It's not your
fault," I whispered. My hands came up to cover my mouth.
   "I know!" she cried.

And now I don't remember what she did. All I see is her frail child's body in a pink bathing suit, her voice like one who knew no darkness, as though darkness existed only beyond her.

"I know!" she said again, let us pretend, and then the rabbit was gone and so was she.

Apple

And what if the organ, dead, worked its way to the outside of the body, worked its way through the skin to surface like a sliver of wood? If the body can generate life, why not regenerate? Plucked like an apple—torn away—leaving the skin paler and pink hued, a scar to mark its deliverance. Here is my old heart; I've grown one anew. We would stretch out our hands and give thanks; we would let it dry and hang it from a string above the baby's cradle. Let the dog play fetch with it. We would leave it in a shoebox in the closet and find it years later, only to wish we had given it away already.

Son

It is autumn and we are all grown up, my siblings and me. In the yard out back I sit with my son, nearly two years old. He picks the burdock I have told him not to pick, one stuck already in his downy red hair. I watch him, my love unrestrained, fiercely protective of this one life, and yet weary in the way one who has learned to distrust her instincts grows weary.

Sky

The sky is blue and the clouds catch there. They are smoky and bone white. Their edges light up like neon signs. I close my eyes and listen. I hear the geese honking in the distance, a screeching like children in the schoolyard. But when I open my eyes I can't see them—not yet. This strange honking comes to me like something from another time, like nothing of this time, time-out-of-time, in the space of this era where we touch each other not with hands, hold each other not with voice, where we kill each other not with gun but—a body shucked, limp on a screen. A body breathless and alone in the dark of a bedroom, the gun turned the wrong way.

Nothing remains of what I held true as a child.

> First used as a term for soldiers, *nostalgia* meant homesickness.
> It is a longing for home,
> the home of memory,
> a place to which one can never return.

Geese

The geese are afloat now in the sky; beautiful, black bodies fly there in pitched arch. I hold my son in my arms. He points with small hands. I don't know what he sees as he cries out. But he is pleased. Later we will roll in the grass and he will jump on me again and again, screaming with bodily pleasure, wild with exhaustion.

Immunity

I am always trying to get at something that exists, rests, lives, just around the bend. Trying to unearth the secret pain so that I might examine it, give name to its spiny features, and sing it back to sleep. There were years when I lost everything. But they passed.

We believe in our immunity, that our privilege vaccinates us from caring about the dead, lost, imprisoned, stolen, or enslaved. Not those somewhere else, those over there, but right here—the invisible ones. And our children—*God, our children*—they cannot be here in this paragraph too. How many times I have prayed over mine, *Please, don't take him from me. I beg of you.* Who suffers in exchange for our freedom? Whose children if not ours? Let us forget that I have said this.

———————

Dead organs make their way to the skin, memory of what has been. There is the golden field where you walked with your sister under the balled-up sun—can you hear the wheat swish in the prairie wind? And there are the days you lay among the statues with your lovers, promising never again. You will pluck the lonely fruit or let them fall on the loamy earth and become fertilizer.

Let us pretend that the body regenerates anew. We will covet what is rightfully ours—our memory, our longing, our home, our money, our children, our freedom. We will return from war to the world we imagined while we sat safely in rooms making robots do our killing. All of our wounds sewn shut like the mouths of the dead we left behind. Let us pretend.

Bird

In her hands, a dead bird, cupped there as she flees. Its feathers catch fire in the light. Nothing really is as it seems to be here, in the quiet of the world. Beneath a sky of gunmetal gray, the baby sighs in my arms, and sleeps and dreams.

Sorrow Is a Mother

I stand in the lake, ankle deep, looking up at the trees. My two children grab hold of my thighs and pull at my swimsuit. Morning time. Words come out of the sky: from clouds, from the wind, from the new green of spring, from the awful dirt-sand of the beach where the children will not let me alone. Color is like sound this time of day. Words unfurl from the green fish of trees, hook and stitch at the crux of my body while last night's moon still hovers there in the shadows.

As a mother, it is not good to complain or to brag unless you find another mother who is willing to be honest with you. She will offer her woes and cry into a cup of tea with you as the children ram furniture like beasts, pull down the curtains, pour liquids into the cracks of the sofa and your shoes. There are public rules of presentation for mothers: you must be firm but not too stern, your children should behave but speak up, they should say hello to strangers but not the strange ones. Never yell at your child in public, although you may scream if imminent danger presents itself. Children should be clean but allowed to get dirty and muddy because, you know, it's good for them. They should never hit or call names or not share, they should never throw stones or sand or sticks or water, and they should offer toys to other children, even random ones on the beach. They should never ever climb up the slide.

Careful, careful, careful, we call to our children when others are looking. But what does *careful* mean to a child? A sound sputtered while she exerts and exudes herself on the monkey bars, dah-dah, like keys played or chords plucked or the song of a bird heard from the nursery window. Careful, I say, because then when he falls I will feel less negligent though falling is a normal part of childhood and something I do not discourage, in theory.

Is it only safe to speak about the children to my husband or our mothers or these other women confidantes? I can't be certain what I should and should not tell. It is the same with feminism, I sometimes think. "I am not a good feminist," women whisper.

I always thought I would have daughters. I never dreamed of two sons. I wanted to teach a daughter about feminism and womanhood, to teach her to shoulder the weight of the world, the sorrow etched into her body, even at birth. I suppose I may have asked too much of a daughter. May have demanded her allegiance and refused to lead by example, as I am apt to do. Now, in the day's ripe morning, I ask myself this question: What is the feminism of motherhood?

As a young woman, when I first learned the concept of feminism, I wielded it like a blunt club in my hand, a thing to wallop over the heads of men and ignorant women, the kind that announced blithely how their best friends were men and they couldn't stand "bitchy women." How I loathed such women; yet, how well I knew them because I too saw that certain men could be easily manipulated. Acutely attuned to the force of misogyny, the way my body was broken down into parts, the way I was taught silence and loyalty and self-betrayal simply by virtue of my birth, why wouldn't I wield what little power I could? How could I have known the price?

Yet I grew up surrounded by strong women and felt safest among these women with whom I could talk openly about my ideas, fears, hopes, and dreams. I sometimes tried out these ideas on men, alone with them in the pine forests of my youth. Parked in pickups or rusty sedans, drinking cases of beer or dark bottles of rum and whiskey, smoking cigarettes and looking up at the boughs of these majestic trees, I'd explain why I felt cheated. I'd explain the dreams I had of change, of justice. Mostly they felt obligated to argue but some were silent and others kissed me.

Men appeared grotesque to me at times—their bodily functions lauded and pleasured. Though, of course, I had been taught as a woman to erase and disguise the so-called coarseness of the flesh—to shave off, paint over, dye, cut, and starve away.

In high school my friends and I drank vodka in the middle of the day and ran naked into the water at a boy friend's cabin as a way to escape from the order of things, and boredom. We thought we'd quickly slip beneath the surface. But it was shallow for yards and yards and finally we collapsed into the knee-deep water in a fit of laughter. Back then there was nothing I loved more than the first fire of booze streaming through me.

Now my feminism slips through my fingers, a scalpel to be used with care, to cut apart mostly my own flesh, to cut open the old wounds and restitch them to fit the softening of my limbs, to give order and meaning to what was once a rush of pain, a flume of shame. But of course, it is hard to unlearn anything so deeply traced, so perfectly entrenched.

🐦 🐦 🐦 🐦

I am teaching myself not to want, though for years I have been obsessed with the subject of longing. My children are a project in longing, a relinquishing of love's subject into the great world beyond this simple frame.

———————

I only post pictures of my children on social media—occasionally the woods, the lake, something of home. But my children, by far, have become my favored subject. I tell myself it is so that my family, who live far away from me, can see them, but in truth I am enamored with my two sons. Is it arrogance, as they are of me, from me, young enough to not yet feel wholly a force of their own? I see so clearly their beauty like the changing of seasons. I feel threaded to their moods as though their anger tugs at me, invisible fishing wire between two deeply caught hooks. I want to capture something of their souls that needs the land around their body—in that square frame—to speak to the otherworldliness of small children. Or perhaps I need evidence of my sacrifices.

Sometimes poetry, but mostly longing rises from this compulsion toward my children. Poetry is perhaps of the same vein, the same pulse and beat, an extension of what it feels like to be a body in the world, listening.

Today, four-year-old Moses wisely navigates my grumpy mood: avoiding, shifting focus, obsequious, and hushed. My toddler is wild in a way I can't tame and don't want to, as he is my second and last baby. Willem screams and romps, he yells, "No!" and "Roar!" He is a dinosaur and an elf and Little Critter. Today my inadequacy bleeds. I long for elsewhere. I long for silence but also to hold them close, press their cheeks into mine and breathe their orphic scents.

Looking at trees, I think of the way the world is not experienced through words but something else—some concoction of emotion, memory, and touch. The wind in my hair in late spring becomes my girlhood, my first love—a little blue paddleboat, fishing rods and a plastic pouch of sunflower seeds between my tanned legs. The smell of my child's head, before I wean him, encompasses the wild thrust of the heart outside the body, the sleepy months of my

first child's life when I grew into motherhood, the insatiable longing I have for children, the bodily drive I feel to kiss his fat cheeks,
a longing I no longer have for my older son, whose cheeks have
grown less plump.

Some days I am full with words that sing out of me; I write essays in my head all day. I see poems coming out of the porches as
I pass, pushing the heavy double stroller. The color of my oldest
son's hair makes a sentence with the sun, a story with the color of
water, a hymn in the heat flush of cheeks and sandy sweat smell.
These are good days.

I take them to the park. I take them to the beach. I sit in the bath in
my swimsuit playing with plastic elephants. I pretend I'm getting
paid for this. Then I lay face down on my bed in the late afternoon
sun and wait for the toddler-baby to come, to tumble into me with
his soft cheeks and short legs, with his puff of lips and uncut hair.
I am holy in this sun, hallowed by the coming of night, its sancti-
fied silence a division from day. The words of story and essay and
poem come from the lifting curtain, the wind, the sound of their
feet rumbling through the hall to the front door and back again,
waiting for their father to return from his everyday world of work
that begins and ends each day at the same time.

🙢🙢🙢🙢

You don't understand, I want to tell the childless, my body seeks
my offspring when they are not present and this makes me long
for my children more than anything, even as I simultaneously feel
smothered. Some part of me yearns for the toddler, my baby, in
the way I once did lovers. I know when he is no longer a toddler,
when his legs and arms grow into the right proportions, I will not
feel this. Hormones change, my body morphs. This desperate love
dissipates, slips, and finds new homes. But this longing is complex
and cannot be eased with, say, getting a babysitter or a full-time

nanny, because, at times, not being with them is as hard as being with them.

Once when my oldest son was eighteen months, I was sick with a stomach bug at my parents' home. I threw up all night and lay in bed sweating through the day. My mother cared for my son but he still nursed and wanted me. "There's no vacation from motherhood," my mother scolded. I suppose she was joking but I felt shocked at the realization that women were supposed to do the work of mothering on top of all the other work, whether paid or unpaid, sick or not. Did my mother think I needed to be reminded of my obligations? That having a child as a woman meant a lifetime identity shift, a lifetime of judgment about that identity, and the physical, emotional, and psychic burden brought on by the work of mothering. Is it really women who judge each other? Or are we doing the work of patriarchy, inside a system that at every bend works to dehumanize us?

What is the feminism of motherhood? The slippery shame a woman is made to feel as a mother. The *not good enough* of her everyday existence transformed into a defiance by way of a love that pledges faithfully to not judge her own children, to let them live freely of their own will, and to never betray them out of fear of what will happen if they don't conform. But God, do I fail. Have I ever failed at anything more? And yet I am a good mother, good enough.

Feminism is not hatred or blaming of men but the arc of equality for all. Misogyny is a nuanced experience, with no one specific to blame. It is the force and pressure of inheritance, the long history of her body as property and object—mutable and malleable, forced and coerced, and as vessel to be filled. Her sanity questioned. Her postbirth experience institutionalized.

———

After I had my children, there came a summer during which I incessantly asked my own mother how she could have had six children. I believe my words were, "How could you have done this to yourself?" We would be pushing strollers down the dirt road, turning into the driveway, and I'd ask her again. "I just can't believe it!" I might exclaim. I do not recall what she said, perhaps she laughed.

"I don't know. You just do it. It got easier," she might have said. Her voice breezy, having long ago perfected answers to such questions.

A few years after she had her sixth child, my mother returned to graduate school to study counseling. She took a full-time job as a high school counselor my senior year at the same school.

☙ ☙ ☙ ☙

In college, I must have read "The Yellow Wallpaper" a dozen times. Like many young women, I felt insane. Perhaps I nursed my feelings of insanity in that they seemed like a logical answer to me. At the time, I was suffering from a variety of alienating diseases—eating disorders, alcoholism, mental illness. But let me be clear, women have suffered the label of insanity since the dawn of time.

The other day, while I was leafing through new collections of short stories, a group of young women came in to the bookstore. I watched them, smitten by youth and their brazen confidence, the way they touched each other in reflexive intimacy. As a young woman and college student, I was mostly a loner, and though it was never an option for me, I always regret not attending a women's college out East. One pointed to a copy of *The Awakening* by Kate Chopin and shouted joyfully, "That's the book that changed my life!" I smiled. Me too. They passed by me and out of the store, leaving me breathless.

To grow up with people who love you deeply and yet fail to teach you how to survive and thrive as a woman, with people who tell you your feelings aren't true, your body is not your own, your God wants you to obey your husband, everything you feel that is not within the bounds of their known world is wrong, is to be made to feel insane.

Often, I have found the term *gaslighting* in reference to women's experience of the world helpful. Coined from the 1938 play and 1944 film *Gaslight*, staring Ingrid Bergman, in which her abusive, criminal husband tries to convince her she's going crazy, *gaslighting* refers to the tactic of questioning the truth of someone's experience. We are told that our realities are not true, made to feel paranoid, oversensitive, foolish, or insane when we articulate the experience of inequality. Reality morphs into something she no longer recognizes as she begins to internalize this voice and eventually to make it her own. *What is wrong with me?* she begins to ask, and not, *What is wrong with the world?* the more accurate question.

It seems easier just to endure the abuse, which I have noticed certain women do in response to our culture's misogyny and sexism. Initially a way to cope, such endurance becomes unconscious and thus a way of life. I think of an old friend's social media post regarding the Women's March of 2017: "What, honestly, are they marching over?" Many women would rather identify with the dominant social power even if it means self-betrayal over an entire lifetime. There's logic to this and it may in fact be the saner option to a lifetime of resistance, of speaking up for and against, of acting as a truth teller.

※ ※ ※ ※

Moses's skin is white, a pale and porcelain white, translucent almost. His strawberry blond hair has turned wiry and thick. I watch the way he stands with his belly pushed out and arms hooked on thin shoulders; he looks out over the water at a sailboat.

When I am away from the children I long for them. I want to run my hand over their hair—the soft puff of baby blond and the wiry red—to rub their cheeks with my fingers and squish their faces. I want to eat them. And yet I would be lying not to admit to visions of self-harm, feelings of immutable rage some days when we are together for too long, when my patience drains away. Though I will never take these actions, I am not the only parent who has envisioned throwing her child against a wall or running away. I am not the only parent who has in a fit of defeat screamed "help" or "I can't take it anymore" to no one. We are not alone, though it feels this way.

As with other things that have lost their grounding in my life, shifting into amorphous blobs of thought-feeling that namelessly hang from my body, I know that I am still opening to motherhood. Morphing through a state of becoming, letting myself be vulnerable, open, wounded.

༝ ༝ ༝ ༝

In the morning, I sit on the futon with my coffee, black and hot. I am vaguely awake and the light coming in through the window lays a square patch of gold down on the honey wood floor, it cuts shadow like the edges of words, the music of a violin sobbing into laughter. I sip and sip. Sometimes I turn on the radio and listen to the news, especially when the ache in me feels ravaging. The words come out of the shadow, made of the darkest light. What is light? What is darkness?

Why, Moses asks, do some bugs fly and others walk? I don't want to answer this question, even if there were a simple explanation; it seems ruinous in comparison to the delight of his inquiries. I want to hear them, to covet them like lines from the shelter of poetry—lines that cut through all that is soulless and fooled. Just as I like the way Moses used to say the wrong past tense of certain words.

I drinked it.
He runned away from me.
We swimmed in that pool, Mama.

I try to decide if I should define my children in terms of what they are or what they are not. Such definitions are for me alone. Moses is not timid. Moses is bold. My husband says that he is a leader. I say he is stubborn like me. Pigheaded, my people would call it. He only has energy for the things he wants to do, which is my folly also. But we spend hours on the work we love.

I want days of uninterrupted silence, but I fear leaving them too long—what it might do to me, the feeling of grief that covers my body when they are not near me, and the sorrow and shame I tend to nurse. Guilty, guilty, guilty, I often taunt myself. But it is not true. Why should women carry this weight and not men? Whatever we do is never enough. If we stay at home with our children, we're labeled stupid; if we work, we're labelled selfish.

They are both quietly at play, but I am not free to do anything besides clean and listen to the radio. Anything requiring concentration cannot be undertaken. So I sit. I stare at the light. I let the words flutter up—crisp bodies escaping the light. I think of the whiteness of pages and the black frames of letters. I catalog the colors of the room, considering whether they're warm or cool and which might be removed, which enhanced. I walk barefoot down the hall into the kitchen, pour more coffee, and then stare out the kitchen window at the sugar maple in my neighbor's yard. In autumn, it turns a deep and violent red—a color so fierce I want to cry.

Before the children, I wrote in the morning at the edge of dawn. I wrote in the fury of dreams. I wrote when the words came bubbling up, frothy and enraged, and when they didn't come. Before children, rage was not a consideration, though shame has always been—twin forces not to be unwed.

⚜ ⚜ ⚜ ⚜

I have been trying to explain to a friend why people have children. "Why would someone want to do that to herself?" she asks.

"I think it's a sickness, a madness, something to do with the chemistry of the body; it's biology and hormones, and certain people make us want to procreate even more."

"Not everyone feels that way," she reminds me.

"Yes, I know," I say.

I am not trying to convince her to have children. I am trying to remember the way it felt to want children more than anything—to own so singular a desire that I could think of little else. For an entire year I grieved my lack of children like I would the death of someone beloved.

Sometimes I tell her stories about my son pooping. Shitting and letting it fall down onto the floor through the leg of his pants. He stands and looks at it; he must be half-terrified and half-elated that such horror exits his body. She and I run in the heat of spring, sweaty and breathless and sometimes brimming with tears so overwhelmed by our decisions and futures and what we have done. Emboldened by the love for each other we have tended through friendship.

⚜ ⚜ ⚜ ⚜

I have been watching the spring again. Walking through the woods by the river I feel light. My sons throw sticks from a late-night bonfire into the water. Then rice cakes, then tiny slivers of a clementine.

———————

The boys run down the muddy bank and then back to me when they see a boat approaching. It's a small motorboat carrying red buoys. Moses leans into me, Willem sits in my lap. We wave and they wave. We wave again and they call out to us, "Good morning!" This pleases the children immensely.

Sometimes I hear Moses singing, "Ding-dong the witch is dead, the wicked witch." I cringe. I suppose my greatest fear is that he will grow up to hate women without even realizing it. He will grow up in privilege and deny his.

I take the Princess Leia clad in skimpy Jabba the Hutt prisoner clothes, a chain attached to her wrist, and hide it. Sometimes if I find a tiny weapon, the size of a safety pin, I throw it away, though I've stockpiled a cache of these weapons in the kitchen cupboard. While taking vitamins or searching for a snack, I take inventory of my stash.

I tell my husband that teaching children there are "good guys" and "bad guys" in the world, as nearly every children's movie insists, makes them vulnerable to a dangerous fiction. To believe that evil is exceptional and not banal, as the philosopher Hannah Arendt insisted, is to deny evil its humanity. In so doing, we become blinded, for evil is human and what one is capable of we all are. How will we understand that we too engage in this system of oppression?

I lay beside Moses in the dark, telling him about Martin Luther King Jr. Tentatively at first, trying to think of words or phrases that he will understand. "Tell me more about him, Mom," he says. I start again. I explain slavery, the civil rights movement (when blacks stood up for themselves), the death of MLK (a great leader, an American hero), all as though it were in the past, which is the lie of history. I too learned about American slavery and the Jewish Holocaust as anomalies, outliers in an otherwise just system of humanity. One in which we could depend on God for justice and safety. If I were there, my eight-year-old self insisted as she read Anne Frank, I would have hidden the Jews. What other role does a white girl have to play in these historical dramas than savior? Perhaps my son feels the same inclination, the same desire for justice, but if so it is most likely due to pop culture. All the TV shows he watches play out the age-old battle of good guy versus bad guy with the good guy or hero always winning.

In the quiet of the room, Moses touches my arm with the tips of his fingers. His brother sleeps in his toddler-sized bed a few feet away. Moses curls his fingers around the cuff of my hand and asks, "Was it a white or a black that shot him, Mom?" He has ninjas that he identifies as the white one, the black one, the blue, and the green. He does not see skin in the ways I was socialized to see it, in the way he too may one day understand human bodies. But prejudice is an arbitrary catalog of difference.

He is silent now in the dark, the fan whirring white noise meant to keep them from waking too soon. "Mom," he whispers.

"Yes?" I say.

"Mom, are we the whites or the blacks?"

I am caught off guard and for a moment I have stumbled into uncharted territory, which is in fact most of the terrain of motherhood. I tell him, and he replies, "Why do we have to be the whites?"

"I don't know," I say. "It's just how we were born." Because what am I to say? He doesn't want to be the bad guy, which is the heart of the problem in a nation that plunges forward, refusing to formally acknowledge the depths of its wrong, to offer a process of truth and reconciliation for all the horror of a past that keeps on happening. Without amends, will we ever change? Without amends will we ever heal? Like the wealth made of slavery, we inherit this ancestry, we carry it, and thus attempt to cover our shame in oh so many ways.

I once believed that the destruction of women and women's bodies was the primary binary force in our culture: the first wrong, the original sin that held together the entire system of oppression and violence against bodies deemed other. But women of color face both sexism and racism in their lives, and racism makes sexism worse. I wanted to nail down an answer, to pinpoint an original sin, and I was grasping for something that would offer solace like solution. But oppression is anything but simple, anything but easily solved.

We are socialized to create otherness through gender roles; the "us versus them" dynamic is essential to maintaining systems of oppression, which is why a multiplicity of gender identities feels so threatening to patriarchy. Judith Butler wrote that gender is performative, which means it's an act and an action that requires maintenance and that demands we continually perform it in order to uphold it. But also, that our actions create a desired effect, they generate the myth of a concentrated gender, of a concentrated power. In the same way, Claudia Rankine insists that race and racism is performed, and that racism persists because we maintain systems of oppression by acting out whiteness in our daily lives. We are all implicated in this system. But we can open ourselves to the possibilities that exist in conversations that come from love, that open at the crux of vulnerability, and that refuse to create otherness in any human being.

It is easy for white people to point fingers at other whites: you're the racist. But this, while at times necessary, often seems like a form of deflection. (I'm not the racist, you are.) How we respond to wrongdoing is of particular importance in creating justice. If we use the tools of dehumanization—racist scum, piece of shit—we maintain the house of the master and his rules.

Today I understand that my life is easier and safer because I am white, middle class, educated, straight, cisgendered. Though because of my womanhood, my femme body, I know intimately the experience of being hated by one's culture in ways that some individuals refuse to see or understand. I also know that my privilege must be eradicated if we are to live in a truly just world. When, as a white woman, my privilege is called out, it doesn't feel good, but this feeling is a part of privilege, a protection of it, and I can work through it. I can listen, be of service, be an ally. That I have that choice is also a privilege.

Is it sad that my son has to learn the history he will inherit as the next generation of his country in the quiet safety of his room, which exists in a neighborhood so sheltered that children run around after dark, ride bikes on the street, walk home from school without fear? Yes. But only because children make it very clear how different the world could be. Moses walks alone down the block to a friend's house at four years old. His life is easier because he will always be protected by his magic white shield.

I don't yet know how I will teach him to see his privilege and not be blinded by socialization, by his want to not be the bad guy. Or how I will teach him to see hate and remain open to love. I am sure I will fail in many ways; but this is the work of a mother. This is the feminism of motherhood.

꒰꒰꒰꒰

What will become of this incessant urge to kiss my children's cheeks and rub my nose into the unbelievably soft hair, this devastation over tiny feet, this wildfire longing to hold them close

enough to hear the beats of their small hearts, the sound of their
breath as it catches and releases, the patterning of their souls in
certain faces they make? Will I forget the sorrow of a mother
when it is no longer mine? Or will it always be there, morphing
into form after form of longing? What is certain to me is this: my
culture refuses to articulate the truth of motherhood, the reality
of women's lives, the psychic-physical-emotional-mental toll of
mothering in a society that pretends the fact that women grow humans inside of their bodies, birth them, and care for them is anything less than wildly heroic.

The children are playing quietly at the window. My coffee is cold.
Is it late, I think? Is it too late or is it early in this life? If only we
knew—then how would we live, how would we love? Our sacrifices floating like tiny goldfish in a murky stream—so soon forgotten, so easily lost in the tender joy of it all, the radical defiance of
hope.

Made Holy

When you are sober for longer than a phone call, after your mother has died and the cabin has sold, I still won't put your name into my favorites on my phone for fear you'll slip away again. Grandma was always superstitious. When she spilled salt, she threw it over her left shoulder "into the eye of the devil." She never walked under a ladder or let a black cat cross her path. Once you told me it was bad luck to stir my drink with a butter knife and so I've never been able to do it since, though it seems the right utensil for the job. How many times have I held my breath over a bridge, crossed my fingers, knocked on wood? How many times have I lost and found you?

Yours is not my story to tell; I don't know how to save you and I always knew, deep down, that I was the only one who could save myself. It just took a long time to believe I was worth saving. You move between lives and often when you are here I no longer recognize you, or, rather, I can't find the "us" that once existed. I know only how to offer the language of my own recovery and I have learned to love you at this distance. That love can exist in this balm of acceptance, no strings attached, surprises and confuses me at times. But it is not intimacy, nor the closeness of our youth. It's a simple and judgeless love that requires a certain dedication to letting go. A defiance in the face of this disease that it seems will outlive us all.

———

At Christmas, the first without your mother who loved all holidays madly, we cram into my mom's living room. Your hair is cropped and dyed black, your body thin. Our uncle shows up drunk, asking Mom for wine, which she dutifully pours and refills multiple times. His oldest son, sober and about to become a father, shakes his head. But Uncle laughs and rocks in his chair, his blue eyes glisten from his ruddy, weathered face. He has sold his land and given away his house and lives like a monk in a camper on the edge of his brother's property—a trailer we briefly visited when we went to look for him after Grandma died. All we found was a half-empty can of baked beans on the tiny table that attached to the wall.

Only one of your younger but grown-up sisters comes to Christmas, though my mother has roasted two turkeys and spent all Christmas morning cooking. Your son and your sister's husband stay home with your dad. We don't know how to act without your mom here to yuck it up with my mom, to elicit our eye rolls. In recent years, she has shown up high on painkillers, hoping to keep the pain from cancer at bay for a few hours. After the meal, she'd nod off for a bit, wake, and seek coffee from my mother, her big sister.

You give me a book and a scarf you crocheted. I don't have a gift for you. Embarrassed, I hand you a jar of Vermont honey. My second son is only three months; I hope you'll forgive me. Outside you smoke in the cold. In the living room you smile, joke, and drink diet soda from a can. Two summers ago, when your mom was still alive, and you were homeless and out of touch, I lay on the deck in the sun listening to your mother tell me how she had never been an alcoholic. I had heard the story before, so I pressed my eyes closed and pretended to listen. "I was just self-medicating," she said. Her premise rested on the fact that a year or two ago she had drunk a beer in Florida and didn't drink another. Who needs beer when you've got opiates, I cruelly thought. I never learned the names of pain medicine despite the years I worked the counter at my father's small-town pharmacy. Knowing might have been seduction enough.

At Christmas, I watch you examine the veins in your forearms and stroke your inner elbows like one might touch the delicate cheek of a baby. *Is there heroin in heaven?* we will joke, on the first anniversary of your mother's death, two days before her birthday in April. *Heaven is heroin*, I will say. It was this kind of dark humor that had always saved us. I will call to be a comfort but then I push you to talk about the impending sale of the family cabin, even though you don't want to, even though it is probably one of the worst days of your life.

"It's gone," you say to me. There's a lien on your mother's name from outstanding credit card bills, back taxes to pay, and a second mortgage on Grandma's house. No one has that kind of money. There's nothing we can do. But I don't want to lose this refuge of childhood. All my life I have longed to return to the places of my youth and find them unchanged. Now, selfishly, I want to return to the cabin to walk the cement path and trace our handprints, to follow the trail to the fort at the point, to sit out on the deck and look at the murky lake. I want to return so as to believe time can stop, that somewhere we are all again safely alive in the before of our living.

It feels like we're losing your mom again, a second time, and cruelly on the anniversary of her death. It was at the cabin she felt the quiet center of her being open to the world. It is hard to understand exactly why a place offers such comfort, but your mother knew this. Your father always told her that Grandpa wasn't there in those woods and walls and water. But she knew otherwise and every June she returned to stay through August. Place carries with it all our many selves. For your mother, the cabin might have carried her childhood, girlhood, first loves, motherhood, and the people that have since left—her mother and father.

———

About the cabin, your mother once wrote:

> She has at last found what she sought, solitude,
> And it's strangely unreal
> . . . .
> She swims far beneath the surface
> And looks at her hand
> On a cold winter night she will wonder if it was real at all
> She only knows for sure that there is a July

After we hang up I feel ashamed. Like with my children, there are times I want to consume you, to swallow you whole because I can't bear the thought of your pain. Inside my body you will live safely, protected from the world. I worry you're lonely, heartbroken over your now almost-grown-up son's refusal to see you. I fear your loneliness though you tell me you're doing fine, going to meetings, and visiting your sister and her kids.

A week after our phone conversation my mom visits me in Vermont. My family, Mom, and I drive to Boston to watch two of my sisters, Hannah and Sigrid, run the marathon. On her last morning with me we sit drinking coffee in my living room; my two sons play on the floor. Moses keeps asking my mom to join him and though she has spent hours playing dinosaurs and *Toy Story* with him, our morning coffee together is sacred. "Let Amma drink her coffee first," she tells him. My son momentarily relents. I watch him stand at the window—his favorite spot—looking out. He picks up a toy elephant and walks it along the windowsill, slipping easily into his imaginary world. My mom sits in the rocking chair, cross-legged, cupping her mug. "I don't know how to be in the world without my sister," she begins. "I don't want to be sad. I don't want to be angry."

———

I can think of nothing comforting to say. Only words that would mute her feelings come to mind, lies: it will be okay, it will get better. It's raining outside, late April. I don't want to live in that world either, I think.

"I know that I will always miss my sister," she says as though she is only now speaking it out loud. Only now making sense of it all.

"Maybe each stage of grief is meant to last a year," I offer. Though the stages of grief seem like an absurd fairy tale, I also understand the power in naming. I think of a writing assignment one of my first writing teachers gave me in which I wrote about a character going through each stage of grief. I imagined a man watching a tree out his kitchen window. Mourning the loss of his wife to cancer, he shatters a plate, curses the world, hides in their former bed, but he is eventually one day overcome with the beauty of spring as though ambushed by blossoms and for a brief moment he forgets the pain and the hell and the rage. And in forgetting he understands that the grief will slowly heal but the wound keeps her with him, alive in his body, buried and singing spring into being.

Mom and I talk about the flowers she will plant in the garden she will make for her sister this spring or someday. Lupines, she tells me, because she and her sister always wanted to be Miss Rumphius when they grew old, a woman in a children's book, who in order to make the world more beautiful, planted lupines everywhere she went.

⚘ ⚘ ⚘ ⚘

No one had an uncomplicated relationship with your mother. Her intensity, her exuberance (her beauty) was suffocating at times. She made demands, she manipulated other people for what she needed, and she was unbelievably careless with money. There were times that she felt toxic to me and years I avoided her.

One of the last times I spoke to your mom, I argued with her. She'd accused you of stealing her painkillers. It was close to her death and right before she had a difficult surgery. You called me, crying. I should have known better, but I wanted to protect you, to "save" you, and so I called her. When I think back on it now, I feel ashamed. "Emily," she spoke my name as though I were a long-lost friend getting in touch. And I was a lost friend, a friend gone astray. Perhaps I couldn't cope with the reality of dying. It's exhausting to die of cancer. Or I couldn't deal with the effects of her painkillers or I resented that she denied her own alcoholism. But probably I identified too deeply with her. It was like looking at a magnified version of my own flaws, insecurities, self-destructive behaviors, and intensity. The desperate need to feel loved that so easily seesawed into depression because no human being could fill that emptiness.

Why hadn't I made conversation with her? Asked how she was doing. Told her I missed her. Asked her if she had written any poems lately. Why hadn't I listened as she told me about her life, her grandchildren, her memories? Instead, I accused her of taking too many pills, of getting high and losing track of how many she'd taken. "Don't be like this," she said, her voice weary. She had always been a second mother to my siblings and me.

I spoke to her once more before she went into surgery, a surgery she survived but pushed the end closer, her body ravaged with cancer. "I'm going to make it through this," she said on the phone, in a voice laden with exhaustion. Throughout the six years she lived with inflammatory breast cancer she had always wanted to fight. "I'm going to be okay," she said, though the doctors were asking her questions about life support and her advance directive. I told her that I loved her. "I love you too, honey." I can still hear the way she said "honey," feel the warmth of that word from her mouth wrapping itself around me. Oh, honey.

———

"The dead do not resent us," my friend told me when I regretted the conversation I'd had with my aunt. A minister, she has been my mentor for years. "They're not in that sort of place." Still, I felt inconsolable when I thought of it.

What do the dead want from us? I wondered. Once, my father, processing the death of his father, said, "No one really remembers you. Even if you are famous." What is it about the living that makes us want to be forever alive in the minds of the world? Why is it so hard to accept that once we're dead, we're done? It can't matter anymore. All of life, some say, hinges on death, and of course it's true in a way. "We were born to die," my husband quips, quoting the singer Lana Del Rey. "It's beautiful," he insists.

☽☽☽☽

The liquor store was just three blocks from Grandma and Grandpa's house in Hibbing, Minnesota. Once my sister Hannah and I walked barefoot with Grandpa to buy beer. She was wearing a pink tutu, as we had been in the middle of a game of dress up. Grandpa carried the case of beer home and we followed, traipsing behind him like our own mini theater troupe.

Grandpa had carried the dead in the Second World War. He dropped out of high school in North Dakota at seventeen to join the navy. The government offered high school diplomas to boys who signed up for service in lieu of their senior year. Sometimes I wonder what he thought of Hiroshima; he never would return to the South Pacific, refusing to take Grandma to Hawaii. Back stateside after the war, he may have spent some time in San Francisco as a carpenter or in a hospital.

How could a child walk the death fields of war and then go home? Who are we to ask this of our beloved? The summer he died of cancer, your mother read Russian novels and lost herself to wine. I cherish this line from your mother's writing because I too lost myself to wine and grief. Perhaps sorrow is a form of heritage, something passed in the DNA, in the blueprint of the body; it remains generation after generation. Perhaps trauma lives longer than the body and *the half-life of love is forever.*

You were always myth and mirror for me—fierce and strong to my oldest cousin bossy pants. You screamed at your father in the yard at the cabin, who knows what it was over, but he could be relentless in his rage, taking you by the throat, pushing you into the stairwell to the loft, his face red and you silent in defiance, triumphant. You pierced your ears half a dozen times in each and gave yourself tattoos, things I would never do for fear of retribution from my parents. But you knew your body was your own or maybe you had already given it up. You could hold your breath until your face turned blue to get your mom off the phone—this always impressed me. You taught yourself to smoke cigarettes and kiss boys and run away from home. You were dangerous, and though I was bold, I felt timid beside you, but we both nursed the same anguish—the death field of the mind that, try as we would, the material world would never heal. Long before I ever took a drink, I was an alcoholic, as were you. It was there in the bloodline, and when I finally figured this out it was like learning we had descended from royalty.

࿓ ࿓ ࿓ ࿓

In Boston, the night before Patriot's Day, my mother and I take the T. We are there to watch my sisters run the marathon. My seven-month-old son, Willem, is strapped to my belly and screaming as we change lines three times and then hop a bus. I'm angry with my mother because she didn't offer to get a taxi. I cannot afford a taxi, I reason, so I cannot suggest we get one that she pays for. This is the way my mind works—resentments form based on what I think people should do. In misery, I crave someone to blame.

Later, after she's left, I regret my anger. I think of you and feel ashamed. You would give anything for an hour on a crowded train with your mother. What would you ask her? What could she say? Or would you simply lay your head against her and breathe in the scent of her body, let her hold you again in that way only a mother can. Someday I will wish for this night back again too. I will long to sit shoulder to shoulder with my mother, my baby screaming in my lap until I latch him to my breast and he sucks fiercely as though starved. The worst day with my mother won't compare to the first day I have to live in a world without her.

Sometimes I see how like your mother you really are: a bit of a loner and a fighter, a lover of life and people, but most of all, a fierce-hearted survivor. Despite the world, you keep on. Perhaps you have accepted the broken nature of all things. God could not otherwise be. It wasn't this brokenness we drank over, but the shame we were made to feel from being broken.

We say that our flaws are what make us human. But we are the only marred creatures of earth, the only ones who believe in sin, and who make gods of our suffering. Yet without suffering what would we be? How would we find each other in all this darkness?

In the cemetery at our grandmother's funeral, the minister spread sand in the shape of the cross over her casket to symbolize the nature of life and death—from dust to dust—and you and I and all our sisters took a pinch of that sand and threw it over our left shoulders, into the eye of the devil. I was sober a year when she died, and you had just left treatment for the first time.

Years have passed since that day we threw sand into the wind and let it scatter. I am holding on to you this time if only in my mind: crossing my fingers, avoiding ladders, and holding my breath over bridges we once traveled together. How else will we be made holy? I sometimes wonder. Unless, of course, we were born that way.

Woodland Bound

In the summer, my husband, two sons, and I drive cross-country to my parents' home on a lake in northern Minnesota. They live in a log house, decorated like a lodge. The boys insist on swimming naked in the shallow water of the lake. Though I worry over their pale skin burning, it seems a pleasure I can't deny them. They are four and almost two years old. I know that soon enough they will grow wary of their nakedness and stumble into that moment of physical shame that so often coincides with an emotional turning inward—the body simultaneously becoming a thing to be hidden and a hiding place.

Late in the afternoon I run the forest trail alone. The pines in the field have grown since last summer; the brush has begun to fill in around them. Soon the field will turn to forest and I will lament the erasure of this open space where bees pollinate and dragonflies hover. Wildflowers abound here: bull thistle, aster, and common yarrow. Harebells hang their dainty purple heads as though in sorrow. Gumweed and black-eyed Susans congregate amid my favorites, which are just beginning to bloom: the common mullein, a hardy flower that looks like a torch, its leaves as soft as flannel. When I stand beside one it reaches the tip of my nose. They can grow eight feet tall. Some believe this native European plant protects against evil spirits and acts as a guardian to the lost.

In the distance, a flood of oxeye daisies gathers like fresh snow. I turn and run into the thick woods for a short stretch; the grass grows to my knees here. I crush clover beneath my feet. The smell of pine presses close. I clap my hands now and then to ward off the bear recently sighted along the trail. But I am not worried. Alone on this trail in the summer heat I turn to mist, breath, sound of footfall, echo of clapping hands. My body becomes a litany of light angled through trees with a near religious dedication to grasping beauty. The trail turns to sand and curls on toward the rows of planted pines I estimate to be forty-year-old growth. Little brush grows beneath these pines; rather, the floor of the forest here is mossy or thick with blueberries growing in shallow clumps. Always a blackbird or robin here, lifting from ground to branch to raspberry bramble as though urging me to follow her in, and I have walked slowly beneath these pines with my baby son and my sister, when she was nine months pregnant with her daughter. We wandered off the trail together. My sister, so close to birth, seemed shrouded in a numinous glow.

⁂

As an adolescent girl, I hid so much from my parents and the world that hiding became a part of me—a comfort, really. I nursed sullen shames and secret disobediences. Painting my face with skin-toned cream from my mother's bathroom drawer became a private ritual of summertime boredom—a secret, as well as a way of hiding the dark circles that already bloomed under my young eyes. The smell, a sharp-scented perfume, and glow of my skin delighted me. I loved also to smell my grandmother's cold creams or to touch the various bottles of pink-hued nail polish in her mirrored cabinets. But there was more than just this. More too than secret cigarettes smoked during lunch break while driving the back roads out of town or stolen jars of mixed booze—a little from each bottle in someone's parents' liquor cabinet—sipped in the back seat of cars or around a bonfire beside the open-pit iron ore mines of my hometown. I wanted a secret life, silent as the trees to which I spoke stories, tale after tale featuring young women and adventure. Now I detect this compulsive itch to imagine in my four-year-old son when he hushes as I near and turns away, irritated by the interruption of his private world.

My husband, a kindergarten teacher, calls it creative play: stories acted out, scenarios conceived, often fears mollified in the process, a certain relief attained. I have my own version of this—stories that come as I run, unravel with a force all their own. Perhaps story is of the body, homed there in the flesh, waiting. As children, we must have known the way the body, and thus the self, belonged to the natural world or to solitude.

The poet Mary Oliver writes of three selves: the childhood self, the social self, and the otherworldly self. This last self exists beyond time. "It," she writes, "hungers for eternity." Children, I would argue, live attuned to the otherworldly self, particularly when allowed to grow bored. Reality and imagination coalesce in their young minds. In adults, the otherworldly self comes most readily to the artist and it, Oliver argues, prefers open spaces and solitude; it concerns itself with the edge of life, the periphery, a place of formlessness and uncertainty—a place that in me feels acutely alive and aware while running this forest path, through the landscape of my youth.

Now, as I run, story lifts its wild heart from the tress, stringed together on the wings of blackbirds, of berries, of dreams.

❧ ❧ ❧ ❧

We abandoned our part-time jobs as baristas, bar maids, hostesses, vegetable farmers, landscapers, nannies, lifeguards, and retail specialists. We left behind our full-time jobs as painters and sculptors, poets and essayists, puppeteers, musicians, and circus performers. We left town for a country of prairie grass and junipers, of oceans lapping deserts, of great islands of sand and sunset. We took our children, wrapped against our backs, cuddled in wagons and wheelbarrows, walking at our sides. We left our cars in the streets with the windows rolled down and the keys in the ignition. We left our credit cards and tip money, our rolls of cash and bank accounts; we left our designer jeans, red lipsticks, and shaving creams that smelled of cinnamon and shoe leather and lavender; we left our student loans and master's degrees. We carried dried beans, loaves of bread, books as old as grandmothers. We packed knives and wooden bowls, blocks of butter and bottles of virgin oil. We carried hatchets and spades wrapped in burlap.

As we walked, our hair grew long and our children dirty. Our hands became strong and our fingernails hardened. We found forests of fir with moss floors where we lay our heads and our babes to sleep. We listened to the owls cry in the night and held each other in a different way, from a different fear—corporeal yet transcendent. Our children curled into us and sighed in their sleep and we dreamed of great mountains with rushing streams filled with fish. We dreamed of the untethered ocean, strong like a god. We dreamed of a home somewhere deep in the earth, thick with the smell of mud and grass, with vegetation, where we lived women and men in collusion, green as earth. Round and happy with need.

We had read Thoreau and the Nearings; we had read *A Sand County Almanac* and *Silent Spring* and Rita Dove and Adrienne Rich. We believed in homesteading and self-sufficiency, in wood cabins with saunas beside the pond or the stream or the lake. We longed for gardens and chickens and farms with apple orchards, with trees like the characters of dreams. We wanted our children to live freely of the land and we knew it would be hard, but we believed in a better life, as though we might be separate from the rest of the world, free from the need to belong. We believed we could change from the body out, and that sweat and muscle would bloom and bear the fruit of our labor.

We stood in clearings and watched deer; we cried out at the sight
of geese flocking home overhead; we lay at night under the blis-
tering stars of a deeper sky and listened to the wolves howl. We
learned the names of trees and flowers and birds and mushrooms.
We pointed out the constellations we had never been able to see
before and taught our children the old myths and made up new
ones because history felt necessary and imagination vital.

We built cabins on the sides of mountains, barns in the valleys,
and stood in the bluffs naked beside the sea, filled with the sound
of the waves as they crashed and as the water shoaled, filled with
the distance of the horizon, the sky lipping there. Swallows built
their nests in our barns and we welcomed them. Our children grew
strong and wild, romping through the fir forests, the birch groves,
and rivers that coiled through the land as they made their way to
the sea. Fear left us as we stood in pastures beside sheep, on the
tips of mountains looking out letting the world beyond us come in,
move through us, form us as it saw fit. We let the weather dictate
our lives, the sun our sleeping habits, and when we returned to
making art, writing stories, puppeteering, and drama, we felt content with mediocrity, we were lazy with our craft, our sentences
floundered and burst, letters fled the page, women stood on stage
and forgot their lines, and no one cared. Paintings looked like rep-
licas of the depicted and sculptures stood lifeless in the fields. We
had made art of our lives; it was all we needed.

Soon our children grew up and left us for the cities, the wars,
and the streets of commerce. We grew old alone, together. We
walked to the sea and listened to her song when our eyes no longer
worked. We lay down on the moss of the fir forest and waited for
the owls to cry out, for the sound of the wolves howling, full with
longing. Naked, we found wonderment in our bodies, old as they
were, and did not want to leave them behind, though we must. We
climbed the mountainside and sat among the wild sheep; they nuz-

zled our furry chins and dry lips and curled up at our sides. We held them. We told each other stories of how we had made this life, of who we were. The night dropped like water spilling and when we slept we dreamed of our children, full and round like the moon, sleeping in tiny rooms in the city, driving cars and riding subways, sitting in cubicles dressed up in neck ties and heels, sipping cocktails with red-eyed green olives and lime wedges after eight-hour days, kissing and making babies, and filling their bank accounts with numbers under a smoggy sky, filled with angst and love and hope and dreams of their own.

🌿🌿🌿🌿

Now in the woods, running, I recall not so much the specifics of my imaginary world as a child but the feeling of joy that arose from the industry and purpose of play, and the knowledge that grownups would not understand. In this same way, I create a litany of beauty as I run this trail—a flower gone to seed stands in solitude, its white orb on the cusp of flushing in the wind, perhaps I will be the last to see it. The smell of pine like a sweet, brisk honey, the give of the sand beneath the sole of my foot, the lift and bounce of the blackbird alight with mischief. I leave the woods and turn back toward home, running the paved road past my sister's house, past a couple in their late sixties crouched in the blueberry patch. My body turns inward, thoughtless in physical meditation, slick with sweat, and breath heavy.

🌿🌿🌿🌿

Odysseus, in the Greek myth, allegedly carried a mullein stalk to ward off the sorcery of Circe, who turned others into swine. The Romans dipped mullein in tallow and carried it as a torch in funeral processions; American Indians may have laid the soft leaves of the mullein in the soles of their shoes. Perhaps I am drawn to the myth of this stalk flower torch, its yellow rosettes of light and wooly leaves, its angular disruption of the northern territory. Or can I sense the way they stand apart from the landscape, not quite belonging? In them my secret selves find a momentary home—the otherworldly selves that want to live in, and indeed arise from, the physical world.

And here is what I sometimes wonder: do we make art from this feeling of apartness, separation and discontent with the social self, the social world? Is our work an attempt to assuage this wound of dividedness by giving life to the force of the imaginary? Or, are we made to feel apart because we are born with the composition of this artist self: malcontent, forward looking, bored if not horrified by the triviality of the mundane routine of abstract commerce, dead-end consumerism. Born rebels, as though bone and breath defy conformity. And how do we reconcile these many selves? How does the girl made of secrets marry this woman running and sing into being her forest litany?

The light is carving out the road; all the magic in the world rests there in the shadow. I record each observation without words— seeded in the body. Each secret beauty caught and held summons prayer that tugs at the knotted coil of my grown-up self—quelling angst, soothing worry, anointing me again in the mystery of all that is possible.

Acknowledgments

The following essays (sometimes slightly altered) appeared in the following publications:

"Self-Portrait," *Rumpus*, November 2017.

"The Blue Room," *American Literary Review*, Spring 2015.

"The Birds" as "The World Is Lucky with Birds," *Mid-American Review* 33, no. 2 (2013).

"Prayer for the Woman Murdered in My Neighborhood," *Normal School* 8, no. 1 (2015). Reprinted by permission of The Normal School, copyright 2015 by Emily Arnason Casey.

"Looking at a Photograph of a Deer Head," *Prick of the Spindle* 8, no. 2 (2014).

"Laughing Water," *upstreet* 9 (2013) (received a "notables listing" in the *Best American Essays* series 2014).

"Alchemy of Shadow," *Hotel Amerika*, 2016.

"Ultima Thule," *South Loop Review: Creative Nonfiction and Art* 15 (2013).

"Reverence Song," *Sonora Review* 64/65 (2014).

"Beneath a Sky of Gunmetal Gray" as "On Nostalgia," *New Delta Review* 5, no. 1 (Fall/Winter 2014).

"Woodland Bound," *Windmill: The Hofstra Journal of Art and Literature* 3 (2018).

Thank you to Walter Biggins for wanting to publish this book and for your insights through many rounds of edits. To my peer review readers, Nicole Walker and Sonja Livingston, for your unsparing and honest critique of my work, and your kind words. Thanks to the editorial board at the University of Georgia Press's CRUX series and the many other amazing people who have worked on this book—I feel so lucky.

Thank you to Maria Damon, my first and most extraordinary writing teacher: you changed my life. To Brian B. for inspiring me to write and for your friendship over the years in humor and readership. To Jenny, my poet twin, for your friendship and the hours of café scribbling we shared: you were my first inspiration.

To my Vermont College of Fine Arts family, there are so many of you, for inspiring the best in me and helping me to see that I could do this: Abby Frucht, Philip Graham, Robin Hemley, Dave Jauss, Ellen Lesser, Patrick Madden, Sue Silverman, and Robert Vivien. Thanks to Andrew and Adam for your friendship, encouragement, and necessary humor in the early days. Thank you to Sarah Twombly, Sarah Seltzer, and Sarah Braud for your love. You make everything okay, always. Thanks to Ben Woodard at *Atlas and Alice Magazine* for your support and editorial genius at the journal, I loved every year of it. Thanks to Laurie Easter for reading these essays and offering endless insight, for showing me how to be brave, and for laughing with me. Especially thanks to Jericho Parms, who read every one of these essays in their earliest forms and this manuscript multiple times, and who has talked me through all the hard stuff. Your friendship and readership have meant the world.

Thank you, Laura, magical creature, for always insisting I honor my gifts and for talking me through it all. Thank you, Vanessa, geode extraordinaire, for listening to me talk about this book on runs for years. For Katherine, my mentor and spiritual guide. For Hillary, my virtual running buddy (meditation, motherhood, and Alice Munro). Thanks to Lois for your wisdom and support and for talking about books with me for an entire decade! For Grace, wise woman, your friendship means so much. Thanks to Wylie for teaching me how to be an artist-mother human, I miss our duplex days. Thanks to Jen B. for conversations on art, life, and love. To my in-laws, thanks for caring for our children so often and for all you do to keep us afloat. I am indebted to all the caretakers and teachers who love my children when I am elsewhere, thank you.

Gratitude to my family for your love, acceptance, joy, and encouragement. To Hannah and Sigrid for reading the manuscript and offering your perspective and vision. To Aden for tolerating that one essay that makes you seem weird and for your endless kindness. To Bess for your presence of mind during many hours of insane child-rearing in a multifamily setting, and Alida for your sense of humor and faith. Thank you to Karissa for being on this journey with me—stay close, stay true. To my Auntie who always lived her best life despite the hardships, you inspire me every day. Many thanks to Grandma Betty for showing me the will of a strong woman. To the women in our family who came before and who will follow, may you know your own truth and keep it always. And to my grandfather—mystery that you are—may your spirit rest easy.

To my mom and dad who instilled in me a love of reading, books, nature, travel, and free time, your mentorship has made all the difference. I love you dearly.

Moses and Willem, thank you for making life amazing, challenging, and crazy every day. I am becoming my best self because of you. Thanks to my love, Josh, for making dinners, packing school lunches, doing the laundry, keeping your creative dreams alive, and loving me exactly the way I am. You are my first reader, most honest critic, and favorite songwriter. Your love and support make everything possible in this life together.

To those still sick and suffering with the disease of alcoholism and addiction, this book is for you: you are loved, you are needed, you belong here. Seek help until you get what you need. You don't have to drink today.

Notes and Sources

The book's epigraph is taken from Judith Kitchen's *Only the Dance* (Columbia: University of South Carolina Press, 1994).

Ancestry of Illness

Song lyrics from Ray LaMontagne's "Beg Steal or Borrow," *God Willin' and the Creek Don't Rise* (2010) and quoted material from Terry Tempest Williams's *Refuge: An Unnatural History of Family and Place* (New York: Vintage Books, 2001).

Self-Portrait

Quoted material from John Berger's *Ways of Seeing* (London: Penguin Group, 1972).

The Blue Room

Quoted poems are from T. S. Eliot's *Four Quartets* (1944; repr., London: Faber and Faber, 1999) and Bill Holm's *Playing the Black Piano* (Canada: Milkweed Editions, 2004).

Prayer for the Woman Murdered in My Neighborhood

Lines quoted from Louise Erdrich's *Love Medicine* (New York: Harper Collins, 1993).

Looking at a Photograph of a Deer Head

Reference made to Andrea Modica photographs from her portfolio *Landscapes*.

Laughing Water

Quoted poem from Ezra Pound's *The Cantos* (New York: New Directions, 1950).

Alchemy of Shadow

Reference made to Andrea Modica photographs from *Pastoral* 5 (2007).

Reverence Song

Quoted poem from Galway Kinnell's "Under the Maud Moon," *The Book of Nightmares* (New York: Houghton Mifflin, 1971).

Body of Memory, Phoenix of Time

Wendy Vogel, "Material Masquerade," *Modern Painters* 27, no. 6 (2015); Virginia Woolf, *Moments of Being,* 2nd ed. (Orlando: Mariner Books, 1985); and "Xu Bing's *A Book from the Sky*," Culture Shock, accessed September 2013, http://www.pbs.org/wgbh/cultureshock/flashpoints/visualarts/xubing .html.

Philip Larkin, "Dockery and Son," *Collected Poems* (New York: Farrar Straus and Giroux, 2004).

Beneath a Sky of Gunmetal Gray

Epigraph from Lia Purpura's essay "Against 'Gunmetal'" in her collection *Rough Likeness* (Louisville, Ky.: Sarabande, 2011).

Sorrow Is a Mother

Judith Butler, *Gender Trouble* (New York: Routledge, 1990) and Claudia Rankine, "In Our Way: Racism in Creative Writing," *Writer's Chronicle*, October/November 2016.

Made Holy

"The half-life of love is forever" is borrowed from Junot Diaz's short story "The Cheater's Guide to Love," *This Is How You Lose Her* (New York: Riverhead Books, 2012).

Woodland Bound

Mary Oliver, *Upstream: Selected Essays* (New York: Penguin Press, 2016) and Maria Popova "The Third Self: Mary Oliver on Time, Concentration, the Artist's Task, and the Central Commitment of the Creative Life," Brain Pickings, https://www.brainpickings.org/2016/10/12/mary-oliver-upstream -creativity-power-time/.

REFERENCE